# Adoration and Proclamation
# Prayer Book

Scripture quotations, unless otherwise noted as "ESV", "NKJV" or "AMP" are taken from the New American Standard Bible, Copyright © 1960, 1962, 1963, 1968, 1971, 1972, 1973,1975, 1977, 1995 by The Lockman Foundation Used by permission. (www.Lockman.org)

Scripture quotations marked "ESV" are from The Holy Bible, English Standard Version (ESV), copyright © 2001 by Crossway, a publishing ministry of Good News Publishers. Used by permission. All rights reserved.

Scripture quotations marked "NKJV" are taken from the New King James Version®. Copyright © 1982 by Thomas Nelson, Inc. Used by permission. All rights reserved.

Scripture quotations marked "AMP" are taken from the Amplified® Bible, Copyright © 1954, 1958, 1962, 1964, 1965, 1987 by The Lockman Foundation. Used by permission. (www.Lockman.org)

Scripture quotations marked "NIV" are taken from the THE HOLY BIBLE, NEW INTERNATIONAL VERSION®, NIV® Copyright © 1973, 1978, 1984, 2011 by Biblica, Inc.® Used by permission. All rights reserved worldwide.

Adoration and Proclamation Prayer Book

© 2015 – Ben Woodward (www.benwoodward.com), Iron Bell Ministries (www.ironbellministries.org)

ISBN-10: 1492225843
ISBN-13: 978-1492225843

For questions about reproduction of this book for bible study, teaching or devotional purposes please email info@benwoodward.com. This book is copyrighted but parts of it may be reproduced with permission from the author and publishers.

0 2 4 6 8 9 7 5 3 1

www.benwoodward.com

www.ironbellmnistries.org

# Contents

**How To Pray Adoration and Proclamation Prayers.**   5
**Adoration**   7
   **Alphabetical List of Attributes**   11
   **Who You Are To Me**   47
**Proclamation**   59
   **God The Provider**   63
   **God The Healer**   67
   **The Pure God**   71
   **The God Who Is For Me**   75
   **The King Of Kings**   79
   **God The Protector**   83
   **A Proclamation Of Faith**   87
   **A Proclamation Of Sonship**   91
   **Who I Am To You**   95
**More Resources**   101

# How To Pray Adoration and Proclamation Prayers.

**1. Find out what God says about Himself.**

The first step requires us to go on a journey of discovery. The easiest way I have found to do this is to ask myself, "What is the biggest obstacle I am facing at this point in time?" I open my Bible and find out what it says about that issue or circumstance. What does God say about Himself related to that issue? If, for example, I was faced with the issue of uncertainty regarding the future, I would search the scripture for others that faced that same uncertainty. How did Jacob survive the uncertainty in his life when his brother was trying to kill him? Scripture says that Jacob discovered God as a shepherd. So, in answer to Jacob's question, I would search out the God who revealed himself as a shepherd and who cares for His people just like a shepherd cares for his flock.

**2. Continue by discovering all the other places in scripture that attribute is revealed.**

Find as many places as you can that speak to that circumstance. Using the previous example as an example, what scripture speaks of God as a shepherd? David speaks of God as a shepherd in Psalm 23. Jesus spoke often of Himself as the Good Shepherd. Write down all the times that this attribute is revealed in scripture. This will be the dynamite that you need to break down the walls of doubt that have been built up over years. Not only will you be creating a catalogue of the attributes of God, you will fall increasingly in love with the Bible as a result, because you will see it as a tool to discover Jesus!

**Begin to speak to God about who He is.**

This does not have to be an earth-shattering event. Prayer is simply communication, so let your prayer be simple and real. Do not attempt to set a world record for the amount of time spent in prayer. Begin with what you are able to and read through the scriptures you have written down about the attribute of God you are focused on. When I pray adoration or proclamation prayers, I focus on three things:

1. What does the Bible say about this attribute of God?
2. Where have I seen this attribute in my own life?
3. Where has God shown himself like this in history?

As I pray, I use these guides to form the basis of my prayers. Beginning with the scripture and a particular attribute of God, I begin to tell him who He is.

**Write down the things God is speaking to you as you pray.**

Often, as you are speaking to God about who He is, God will begin to give you a greater level of understanding about the very thing you are praying. As you develop new language and give more time to the place of prayer, God will respond by unlocking new understanding about Himself. This is the journey of discovering God in prayer.

**Always end with thankfulness and a new perspective!**

As we discover who God is, we will discover who we are. This should always lead to thankfulness! Being thankful will keep us out of any bitterness that comes because of delayed answers. Sometimes we do not get immediate answers. But as we discover who He is, we can trust Him because we know He is good. When delay occurs, the answer is to step it up and increase your thankfulness! Thankfulness gives us correct perspective that will enable us to maintain a spirit of expectancy and faith.

# Adoration Prayer

# What is Adoration Prayer?

Our prayer life is meant to be more than just an afterthought or a boring repetitious discipline that we have to fulfill. It should be more than a list of requests or needs that we are presenting to God. Prayer should be a dynamic encounter that leads us into the knowledge of God. If we are to have this type of prayer life, we are going to need to look at prayer in a different way.

*"Enter into His gates with thanksgiving, and into His courts with praise: be thankful unto Him, and bless His name."* Psalm 100.4

Elizabeth Browning was onto something when she wrote, "How do I love Thee, let me count the ways."[1] What if prayer was actually about a finding a place where we can discover who God is?

When you discover who God is, it causes you to fall in love with Him. This fulfills the first and greatest command – to love the Lord with all your heart, mind, soul and strength. Love is the central core that should fuel all our prayers. One of the ways that we can do this is through a model of prayer called "Adoration Prayer."

Adoration prayer is simply put this way, "let me tell You the many ways that I love You." This is more than just listing things about God; it is learning about who He is and falling in love with who He says He is.

Adoration prayer is a tool that you can use to enhance your prayer life on a day-to-day basis. It takes us out of the 'unending list of prayer requests' type of prayer and gives us a way to love Jesus and discover who He is in the process.

**Adoration prayer can be described in three different ways:**

1. **Love Prayer** - it is a language of love. Adoration helps develop a language of love as we stare into what God says about Himself. When we see Him, we fall in love with Him.

2. **Transformative Prayer** - not only do we fall in love with God, we are also changed when we adore God. It is the biblical principle of becoming what we behold. What you stare into, you will become like. Learning about who God is changes who we are.

3. **Enjoyable Prayer** - Adoration prayer gives us an effective tool to be able to enjoy our prayer time. It is a practical way to pray the scripture and to discover who God is. It can be done anywhere and anytime.

When we learn how to adore the Lord, we are saturated in His presence and filled with the word of the Lord. Suddenly all circumstances are seen through the perspective of who God is. We discover the God who leads us, is a shepherd and is a friend – and the best thing is we haven't even asked Him for a thing yet!

We need to return to the place of prayer. It must become the central reality we build our lives upon. Adoration is the gateway to this kind enjoyable, transformative, love prayer. It is the way to an unshakeable

---

[1] How Do I Love Thee (Sonnet 43) – Elizabeth Browning

hope in God. It is the place we discover a deep relationship with Jesus and when we experience it, we find peace and joy.

*"O magnify the Lord with me, and let us exalt His name together." Psalm 34.3*

**Adoration Prayer: the simple steps.**

1. Using your bible or this adoration manual, look for an attribute of God. Always use some form of scripture as the foundation for your prayer. It will help you to stay focused on what God says about Himself, not just what you think about Him.

2. Begin to pray using that scripture as the basis for the prayer. "Jesus, You are the great shepherd. As I look back on my life I can see how You have been a shepherd to me. I love that the scripture calls You a shepherd..."

3. Don't ask for a thing. There is a time for asking, but as you adore the Lord, make sure you focus on loving Him and telling Him who He is.

For a more in-depth teaching on Adoration prayer, check out "You Shall Know The Truth" by Ben Woodward. You can purchase it from www.benwoodward.com.

# Adoration exercise

Simple Adoration Introduction (30 minute exercise)

## Part 1.

1. Take an attribute of God in the "A" section and read the verse related to it aloud.
2. Say this phrase - "Thank you that you are [attribute] to me." That's it! Don't say anything else, don't ask for anything, just say the phrase.
3. Repeat the above steps with attributes from "B" through "G"

## Part 2.

1. Using the same attributes you just used in step 1, think about how God has displayed himself to you in that way.
2. Pray using those same attributes like this - "Thank you that you are [attribute] to me. I remember how you showed me this part of your character [use whatever circumstance you have thought about]."

## Part 3.

1. Look through the list of attributes and find one that has meant a lot to you personally.
2. Begin to thank the Lord for how He met you in that circumstance and talk to him about how much that part of His character means to you.

**The Abba God**
For you have not received a spirit of slavery leading to fear again, but you have received a spirit of adoption as sons by which we cry out, "Abba! Father!" Rom. 8.15

Because you are sons, God has sent forth the Spirit of His Son into our hearts, crying, "Abba! Father!" Gal. 4.6

**The Active God**
He answered them, "My Father is working until now, and I Myself am working." John 5.17

**The Almighty God**
Great is our Lord and abundant in strength; His understanding is infinite. Psa. 147.5

"I am the Alpha and the Omega," says the Lord God, "who is and who was and who is to come, the Almighty." Rev. 1.8

Now when Abram was ninety-nine years old, the LORD appeared to Abram and said to him, "I am God Almighty; Walk before Me, and be blameless. Gen. 17.1

**The God Who Answers Me**
I was crying to the Lord with my voice, and He answered me from His holy mountain. Psa. 3.4

In my trouble I cried to the Lord, And He answered me. Psa. 120.1

Now I know that the Lord saves His anointed; He will answer him from His holy heaven with the saving strength of His right hand. Some *boast* in chariots and some in horses, but we will boast in the name of the Lord, our God. Psa. 20.6-7

**The Approachable God**
But Jesus said, "Let the children alone, and do not hinder them from coming to Me; for the kingdom of heaven belongs to such as these." Matt. 19.14

Let us draw near with a sincere heart in full assurance of faith, having our hearts sprinkled clean from an evil conscience and our bodies washed with pure water. Heb. 10.22

**The Available God**
God is our refuge and strength, a very present (available) help in trouble. Psa. 46.1

Draw near to God and He will draw near to you. Jam. 4.8

**The God Who Is Our Advocate**
My little children, I am writing these things to you so that you may not sin. And if anyone sins, we have an Advocate with the Father, Jesus Christ the righteous. 1 John 2.1

And I will ask the Father, and He will give you another Comforter (Counselor, Helper, Intercessor, Advocate, Strengthener, and Standby), that He may remain with you forever. John 14.16 AMP

**The Avenging God**
Never take your own revenge, beloved, but leave room for the wrath of God, for it is written, "VENGEANCE IS MINE, I WILL REPAY," says the Lord. Rom. 12.19

**The Awesome God**
Who is like You among the gods, O LORD? Who is like You, majestic in holiness, awesome in praises, working wonders? Ex. 15.11

**The God Who Is Aware**
The eyes of the Lord are toward the righteous and His ears are *open* to their cry. Psa. 34.15

**Notes**

### The Better Than God
For a day in Your courts is better than a thousand outside. I would rather stand at the threshold of the house of my God than dwell in the tents of wickedness. Psa. 84.10

Because Your lovingkindness is better than life, my lips will praise You. Psa. 63.3

### The Building God
Unless the LORD builds the house, they labor in vain who build it; unless the LORD guards the city, the watchman keeps awake in vain. Psa. 127.1

For he was looking for the city which has foundations, whose architect and builder is God. Heb. 11.10

### The Bright and Morning Star
"I, Jesus, have sent My angel to testify to you these things for the churches. I am the root and the descendant of David, the bright morning star." Rev. 22.16

### The Beautiful God
In that day the Branch of the LORD will be beautiful and glorious. Is. 4.2

So did You lead Your people [Lord] to make for Yourself a beautiful *and* glorious name [to prepare the way for the acknowledgment of Your name by all nations]. Isa. 63.14 AMP

One thing I have asked from the Lord, that I shall seek: That I may dwell in the house of the Lord all the days of my life, To behold the beauty of the Lord and to meditate in His temple. Psa. 27.4

### Our Beloved God
My beloved is dazzling and ruddy, outstanding among ten thousand. Song 5.10

### The Burden-bearing God
Cast your burden upon the LORD and He will sustain you; He will never allow the righteous to be shaken. Psa. 55.22

Come to Me, all who are weary and heavy-laden, and I will give you rest. Take My yoke upon you and learn from Me, for I am gentle and humble in heart, and you will find rest for your souls.
Matt. 11.28-29

### The Bridegroom God
And Jesus said to them, "The attendants of the bridegroom cannot mourn as long as the bridegroom is with them, can they? But the days will come when the bridegroom is taken away from them, and then they will fast." Matt. 9.15

**The Blessed God**
Blessed be the God and Father of our Lord Jesus Christ, who according to His great mercy has caused us to be born again to a living hope through the resurrection of Jesus Christ from the dead.  1 Pet. 1.3

And blessed be God Most High, who has delivered your enemies into your hand. Gen. 14.20

**The Bread Of Life**
For the bread of God is that which comes down out of heaven, and gives life to the world. John 6.33

I am the bread of life. John 6.48

**Notes**

### The Comforter
I will ask the Father, and He will give you another Helper (Comforter), that He may be with you forever. John 14.16

Shout for joy, O heavens! And rejoice, O earth! Break forth into joyful shouting, O mountains! For the LORD has comforted His people and will have compassion on His afflicted. Is. 49.13

### The Compassionate God
I Myself will make all My goodness pass before you, and will proclaim the name of the LORD before you; and I will be gracious to whom I will be gracious, and will show compassion on whom I will show compassion. Ex. 33.19

You, O LORD, will not withhold Your compassion from me; Your lovingkindness and Your truth will continually preserve me. Psa. 40.11

### The Covenant Keeping God
Know therefore that the LORD your God, He is God, the faithful God, who keeps His covenant and His lovingkindness to a thousandth generation with those who love Him and keep His commandments. Deut. 7.9

He has remembered His covenant forever, the word which He commanded to a thousand generations. Psa. 105.8

### The Conquering God
But in all these things we overwhelmingly conquer through Him who loved us. Rom. 8.37

### The Creative God
When I consider Your heavens, the work of Your fingers, the moon and the stars, which You have ordained… Psa. 8.3

Do you not know? Have you not heard? The Everlasting God, the LORD, the Creator of the ends of the earth does not become weary or tired. His understanding is inscrutable. Is. 40.28

### The Christ (The Anointed One)
Simon Peter answered, "You are the Christ, the Son of the living God. Matt. 16.16

### The Counselor
And His name will be called Wonderful Counselor, Mighty God, Eternal Father, Prince of Peace. Is. 9.6

### The Caring God
Casting all your anxiety on Him, because He cares for you. 1 Peter 5.7

You who know, O Lord, Remember me, take notice of me. Jer. 15.15

**You Are My Confidence**

Trust in, lean on, rely on, *and* have confidence in Him at all times, you people; pour out your hearts before Him. God is a refuge for us (a fortress and a high tower). Psa. 62.8 AMP

[Most] blessed is the man who believes in, trusts in, *and* relies on the Lord, and whose hope *and* confidence the Lord is. Jer. 17.7 (AMP)

For You are my hope; O Lord God, *You are* my confidence from my youth. Psa. 71.5

**Notes**

_____
_____
_____
_____
_____
_____
_____
_____
_____
_____
_____
_____
_____
_____

### The Determined God
For God so loved the world, that He gave His only begotten Son, that whoever believes in Him shall not perish, but have eternal life.  John 3.16

When the days were approaching for His ascension, He was determined to go to Jerusalem.  Luke 9.51

What man among you, if he has a hundred sheep and has lost one of them, does not leave the ninety-nine in the open pasture and go after the one which is lost until he finds it?  Luke 15.4

### The Defender God
For I will defend this city to save it for My own sake and for My servant David's sake.  Is. 37.35

The LORD is my light and my salvation; Whom shall I fear?  The LORD is the defense of my life; Whom shall I dread?  Psa. 27.1

### The Delivering God
My lovingkindness and my fortress, my stronghold and my deliverer, my shield and He in whom I take refuge, who subdues my people under me.  Psa. 144.2

Let the Lord be mindful of me. You are my help and my deliverer; do not delay, O my God.  Psa. 40.17

And so all Israel will be saved; just as it is written, "THE DELIVERER WILL COME FROM ZION, HE WILL REMOVE UNGODLINESS FROM JACOB."  Rom. 11.26

### The God Of Delight
Delight yourself in the LORD; and He will give you the desires of your heart.  Psa. 37.4

The perverse in heart are an abomination to the LORD, but the blameless in their walk are His delight.  Prov. 11.20

### The Dazzling God
My beloved is dazzling and ruddy, outstanding among ten thousand.  Song 5.10

### The God Of Our Desire
As the deer pants for the water brooks, so my soul pants for You, O God.  Psa. 42.1

### The God of all Dominion
Your kingdom is an everlasting kingdom, And Your dominion *endures* throughout all generations. Psa. 145.13

How great are His signs and how mighty are His wonders! His kingdom is an everlasting kingdom and His dominion is from generation to generation. Dan. 4.3

**Notes**

### The Eternal God
"I am the Alpha and the Omega," says the Lord God, "who is and who was and who is to come, the Almighty." Rev. 1.8

Before the mountains were born or You gave birth to the earth and the world, even from everlasting to everlasting, You are God.  Psa. 90.2

### The Essential God
For in Him we live and move and exist, as even some of your own poets have said, "For we also are His children." Acts 17.28

### The Enlightening God
You will make known to me the path of life; in Your presence is fullness of joy; in Your right hand there are pleasures forever.  Psa. 16.11

Your word is a lamp to my feet and a light to my path.  Psa. 119.105

### The Enthroned God
Oh, give ear, Shepherd of Israel, You who lead Joseph like a flock; You who are enthroned above the cherubim, shine forth!  Psa. 80.1

To You I lift up my eyes, O You who are enthroned in the heavens!  Psa. 123.1

### The Excellent God
Having become as much better than the angels, as He has inherited a more excellent name than they.  Heb. 1.4

### Notes

___

___

___

___

___

___

### The "For Me" God
What then shall we say to these things? If God is for us, who is against us… Christ Jesus is He who died, yes, rather who was raised, who is at the right hand of God, who also intercedes for us.  Rom. 8.31,34

Then my enemies will turn back in the day when I call; this I know, that God is for me.  Psa. 56.9

### The Finishing God
Looking unto Jesus, the author and finisher of *our* faith, who for the joy that was set before Him endured the cross, despising the shame, and has sat down at the right hand of the throne of God. Heb. 12.2 NKJV

### The Fountain of Life
O LORD, the hope of Israel, all who forsake You will be put to shame. Those who turn away on earth will be written down, because they have forsaken the fountain of living water, even the LORD.  Jer. 17.13

### The Faithful God
God is faithful, through whom you were called into fellowship with His Son, Jesus Christ our Lord.  1 Cor. 1.9

God is faithful, who will not allow you to be tempted beyond what you are able, but with the temptation will provide the way of escape also, so that you will be able to endure it.  1 Cor. 10.13

Jesus Christ, the faithful witness, the firstborn of the dead, and the ruler of the kings of the earth. To Him who loves us and released us from our sins by His blood.  Rev. 1.5

### The Forgiving God
If we confess our sins, He is faithful and righteous to forgive us our sins and to cleanse us from all unrighteousness.  1 John 1.9

Iniquities prevail against me; as for our transgressions, You forgive them.  Psa. 65.3

### Our Father
Now may our Lord Jesus Christ Himself and God our Father, who has loved us and given us eternal comfort and good hope by grace…  2 Th. 2.16

And I will be a father to you, and you shall be sons and daughters to Me, says the Lord Almighty.  2 Cor. 6.18

### The Fulfilling God
Now the Lord has fulfilled His word which He spoke; for I have risen in place of my father David and sit on the throne of Israel, as the Lord promised, and have built the house for the name of the Lord, the God of Israel. 1 Kings 8.20

I will cry to God Most High, To God who accomplishes all things for me. Psa. 57.2

**The Forerunner (Who Goes Before Us)**

But you will not go out in haste, nor will you go as fugitives; For the Lord will go before you, and the God of Israel will be your rear guard. Is. 52.12

Where Jesus has entered as a forerunner for us, having become a high priest forever according to the order of Melchizedek. Heb. 6.20

**Notes**

### The God Who Guides
You, in Your great compassion, did not forsake them in the wilderness; the pillar of cloud did not leave them by day, to guide them on their way, nor the pillar of fire by night, to light for them the way in which they were to go. Neh. 9.19

For the Lamb in the center of the throne will be their shepherd, and will guide them to springs of the water of life; and God will wipe every tear from their eyes." Rev. 7.17

### The Guardian God
For you were continually straying like sheep, but now you have returned to the Shepherd and Guardian of your souls. 1 Pet. 2.25

### The Generous God
Every good thing given and every perfect gift is from above, coming down from the Father of lights, with whom there is no variation or shifting shadow. James 1.17

For the wages of sin is death, but the free gift of God is eternal life in Christ Jesus our Lord. Rom. 6.23

### The Good God
Beloved, do not imitate what is evil, but what is good. The one who does good is of God; the one who does evil has not seen God. 3 John 1.11

No one is good except God alone. Luke 18.19

### The Great God
Great and marvelous are Your works, O Lord God, the Almighty; Righteous and true are Your ways, King of the nations! Rev. 15.3

Therefore, since we have a great high priest who has passed through the heavens, Jesus the Son of God, let us hold fast our confession. Heb. 4.14

For the LORD is a great God and a great King above all gods. Psa. 95.3

### The Glorious God
Now therefore, our God, we thank You, and praise Your glorious name. 1 Chr. 29.13

### The Good Shepherd
The Lord is my shepherd, I shall not want. Psa. 23.1

I am the good shepherd; the good shepherd lays down His life for the sheep. John 10.11

**The Gift**

Peter *said* to them, "Repent, and each of you be baptized in the name of Jesus Christ for the forgiveness of your sins; and you will receive the gift of the Holy Spirit." Acts 2.38

For since He Whom God has sent speaks the words of God [proclaims God's own message], God does not give Him His Spirit sparingly *or* by measure, *but* boundless is the gift God makes of His Spirit! John 3.34 AMP

**Notes**

### The Holy God
For I am the LORD your God. Consecrate yourselves therefore, and be holy, for I am holy. Lev. 11.44

Exalt the LORD our God and worship at His footstool; Holy is He. Psa. 99.5

And the four living creatures, each one of them having six wings, are full of eyes around and within; and day and night they do not cease to say, "HOLY, HOLY, HOLY is THE LORD GOD, THE ALMIGHTY, WHO WAS AND WHO IS AND WHO IS TO COME." Rev. 4.8

### The Happy God
"You have loved righteousness and hated lawlessness; Therefore God, Your God, has anointed You with the oil of gladness more than Your companions." Heb. 1.9.

He who sits in the heavens laughs. Psa. 2.4

### The Honest God
God is not a man, that He should lie, nor a son of man, that He should repent; Has He said, and will He not do it? Or has He spoken, and will He not make it good? Num. 23.19

### The God Of Hope
The Lord is my portion *or* share, says my living being (my inner self); therefore will I hope in Him *and* wait expectantly for Him. Lam. 3.24 AMP

To whom God willed to make known what is the riches of the glory of this mystery among the Gentiles, which is Christ in you, the hope of glory. Col. 1.27

### The God Who Heals
Jesus was going through all the cities and villages, teaching in their synagogues and proclaiming the gospel of the kingdom, and healing every kind of disease and every kind of sickness. Matt. 9.35

Bless the LORD, O my soul, and forget none of His benefits; who pardons all your iniquities, who heals all your diseases. Psa. 103.3

For I, the Lord, am your healer. Ex. 15.26

### Our Hiding Place
You are my hiding place; You preserve me from trouble; You surround me with songs of deliverance. Selah. Psa. 32.7

**God The Helper**

But I tell you the truth, it is to your advantage that I go away; for if I do not go away, the Helper will not come to you; but if I go, I will send Him to you. John 16.7

**God Our Husband**

For your husband is your Maker, whose name is the LORD of hosts; and your Redeemer is the Holy One of Israel, who is called the God of all the earth. Is. 54.5

**Notes**

# I

**The Innocent God**
God made Him who had no sin to be sin for us, so that in Him we might become the righteousness of God.  2 Cor. 5.21

He was oppressed and He was afflicted, Yet He did not open His mouth; Like a lamb that is led to slaughter, and like a sheep that is silent before its shearers, So He did not open His mouth.  Is. 53.7

**The Incorruptible God**
[They] exchanged the glory of the incorruptible God for an image in the form of corruptible man and of birds and four-footed animals and crawling creatures. Rom. 1.23

**The Incomparable God**
For who is God, but the LORD? And who is a rock, except our God.  Psa. 18.31

Great is our Lord and abundant in strength; His understanding is infinite.  Psa. 147.5

**The Intercessory God**
Therefore He is able also to save forever those who draw near to God through Him, since He always lives to make intercession for them.  Heb. 7.25

**The Immortal, Invisible God**
Now to the King eternal, immortal, invisible, the only God, be honor and glory forever and ever. Amen.  1 Tim. 1.17

**The God Who Instructs**
Know also in your [minds and] hearts that, as a man disciplines and instructs his son, so the Lord your God disciplines and instructs you. Deut. 8.5 AMP

I [the Lord] will instruct you and teach you in the way you should go; I will counsel you with My eye upon you. Psa. 32.8 AMP

**The Inviting God**
Go therefore to the main highways, and as many as you find *there*, invite to the wedding feast.' Matt. 22.9

For the promise is for you and your children and for all who are far off, as many as the Lord our God will call to Himself. Acts 2.39

**The Indescribable God**
Who is like You among the gods, O Lord?  Who is like You, majestic in holiness, awesome in praises, working wonders? Ex. 15.11

**The God Of The Impossible**
For nothing will be impossible with God. Luke 1.37

**Notes**

### The Jealous God
For you shall not worship any other god, for the LORD, whose name is Jealous, is a jealous God. Ex. 34.14

For the LORD your God is a consuming fire, a jealous God. Deut. 4.24

### The Just God
Rejoice greatly, O daughter of Zion! Shout in triumph, O daughter of Jerusalem! Behold, your king is coming to you; He is just and endowed with salvation, humble, and mounted on a donkey, even on a colt, the foal of a donkey. Zech. 9.9

The Rock! His work is perfect, for all His ways are just; a God of faithfulness and without injustice, Righteous and upright is He. Deut. 32.4

### The Joyful God
And He brought forth His people with joy, His chosen ones with a joyful shout. Psa. 105.43

Even those I will bring to My holy mountain and make them joyful in My house of prayer. Their burnt offerings and their sacrifices will be acceptable on My altar; for My house will be called a house of prayer for all the peoples. Is. 56.7

In Your presence is fullness of joy; In Your right hand there are pleasures forever. Psa. 16.11

### Notes

### The King Of Kings
He is Lord of lords and King of kings, and those who are with Him are the called and chosen and faithful." Rev. 17.14

He who is the blessed and only Sovereign, the King of kings and Lord of lords, 1 Tim. 6.15

### The Kind God
Be kind to one another, tender-hearted, forgiving each other, just as God in Christ also has forgiven you. Eph. 4.32

### The Keeper God
The LORD is your keeper; The LORD is your shade on your right hand. ...The LORD will protect you from all evil; He will keep your soul. Psa. 121.5,7

### Notes

# L

### God Who Is A Lamp
For You are my lamp, O LORD; And the LORD illumines my darkness.  2 Sam. 22.29

Your word is a lamp to my feet and a light to my path.  Psa. 119.105

### The Loving God
The LORD appeared to him from afar, saying, "I have loved you with an everlasting love; therefore I have drawn you with lovingkindness."  Jer. 31.3

See how great a love the Father has bestowed on us, that we would be called children of God.  1 John 3.1

For God so loved the world, that He gave His only begotten Son, that whoever believes in Him shall not perish, but have eternal life.  John 3.16

I in them and You in Me, that they may be perfected in unity, so that the world may know that You sent Me, and loved them, even as You have loved Me.  John 17.23

### God The Light
The people who walked in darkness have seen a great light; those who dwelt in the land of the shadow of death, upon them a light [has] shined.  Is. 9.2

Though I dwell in darkness, the LORD is a light for me.  Mic. 7.8

### Notes

_____

_____

_____

_____

_____

_____

_____

### The Majestic God
Who is like You among the gods, O LORD? Who is like You, majestic in holiness, awesome in praises, working wonders? Ex. 15.11

O LORD, our Lord, how majestic is Your name in all the earth, who have displayed Your splendor above the heavens! Psa. 8.1

But there the majestic One, the LORD, will be for us a place of rivers and wide canals on which no boat with oars will go. Is. 33.21

### God Our Maker
Come, let us worship and bow down, let us kneel before the LORD our Maker. Psa. 95.6

Thus says the LORD, your Redeemer, and the one who formed you from the womb, "I, the LORD, am the maker of all things, stretching out the heavens by Myself and spreading out the earth all alone." Is. 44.24

For your husband is your Maker, whose name is the LORD of hosts; and your Redeemer is the Holy One of Israel, who is called the God of all the earth. Is. 54.5

### The Master God
Our only Master and Lord, Jesus Christ. Jude 1.4

His master said to him, "Well done, good and faithful slave. You were faithful with a few things, I will put you in charge of many things; enter into the joy of your master." Matt. 25.23

### The God Of Miracles
God was performing extraordinary miracles by the hands of Paul. Acts 19.11

Then God said, "Behold, I am going to make a covenant. Before all your people I will perform miracles which have not been produced in all the earth nor among any of the nations; and all the people among whom you live will see the working of the LORD, for it is a fearful thing that I am going to perform with you." Ex. 34.10

### The Meek God
Being found in appearance as a man, He humbled Himself by becoming obedient to the point of death, even death on a cross. Phil. 2.8

Now I, Paul, myself urge you by the meekness and gentleness of Christ—I who am meek when face to face with you, but bold toward you when absent! 2 Cor. 10.1

### The Merciful God
When he cries to Me, I will hear, for I am gracious *and* merciful. Ex 22.27 AMP

Therefore, He had to be made like His brethren in all things, so that He might become a merciful and faithful high priest in things pertaining to God, to make propitiation for the sins of the people. Heb. 2.17

Yet in Your great mercies You did not utterly consume them or forsake them, for You are a gracious and merciful God. Neh. 9.31 AMP

**Notes**

# N

**The Near God**
Draw near to God and He will draw near to you. Cleanse your hands, you sinners; and purify your hearts, you double-minded. James 4.8

The kingdom of God has come near to you. Luke 10.9

The LORD is near to all who call upon Him, to all who call upon Him in truth. Psa. 145.18

**The Never Failing God**
He Himself has said, "I WILL NEVER DESERT YOU, NOR WILL I EVER FORSAKE YOU," Heb. 13.5

But I will not break off My lovingkindness from him, nor deal falsely in My faithfulness. Psa. 89.33

Love never fails. 1 Cor. 13.8

**The Always New God**
Behold, the former things have come to pass, now I declare new things; Before they spring forth I proclaim them to you. Is. 42.9

And He who sits on the throne said, "Behold, I am making all things new." And He said, "Write, for these words are faithful and true." Rev. 21.5

**The Nothing Is Impossible God**
For nothing will be impossible with God. Luke 1.37

Behold, I am the LORD, the God of all flesh; is anything too difficult for Me? Jer. 32.27

**The Name Above All Names**
Let them praise the name of the LORD, for His name alone is exalted; His glory is above earth and heaven. Psa. 148.13

For this reason also, God highly exalted Him, and bestowed on Him the name which is above every name. Phil. 2.9

...Far above all rule and authority and power and dominion, and every name that is named, not only in this age but also in the one to come. Eph. 1.21

**The Noble God**
And since we have [such] a great *and* wonderful *and* noble Priest [Who rules] over the house of God, let us all come forward *and* draw near with true (honest and sincere) hearts. Heb. 10.21,22 AMP

**Notes**

### The One and Only God
Hear, O Israel! The LORD is our God, the LORD is one! Deut. 6.4

See now that I, I am He, and there is no god besides Me. Deut. 32.39

### The Overcoming God
These things I have spoken to you, so that in Me you may have peace. In the world you have tribulation, but take courage; I have overcome the world. John 16.33

### The Obedient God
For as through the one man's disobedience the many were made sinners, even so through the obedience of the One the many will be made righteous. Rom. 5.19

### The God Who Owns Everything
The earth is the LORD'S, and all it contains, the world, and those who dwell in it. Psa. 24.1

All things that the Father has are Mine; therefore I said that He takes of Mine and will disclose it to you. John 16.15

### The Omnipresent God
Where can I go from Your Spirit? Or where can I flee from Your presence? Psa. 139.7

### The Outstanding God
My beloved is dazzling and ruddy, outstanding among ten thousand. Song 5.10

## Notes

### God The Perfecter
Fixing our eyes on Jesus, the author and perfecter of faith, who for the joy set before Him endured the cross, despising the shame, and has sat down at the right hand of the throne of God.  Heb. 12.2

### The Preeminent God
He is before all things, and in Him all things hold together. He is also head of the body, the church; and He is the beginning, the firstborn from the dead, so that He Himself will come to have first place in everything.  Col. 1.17,18

### The Protector God
The LORD will protect him and keep him alive, and he shall be called blessed upon the earth; And do not give him over to the desire of his enemies.  Psa. 41.2

The LORD will protect you from all evil; He will keep your soul.  Psa. 121.7

### God The Potter
But now, O LORD, You are our Father, we are the clay, and You our potter; and all of us are the work of Your hand.  Is. 64.8

### God Our Portion
The LORD is my portion; I have promised to keep Your words.  Psa. 119.57

I cried out to You, O LORD; I said, "You are my refuge, my portion in the land of the living."  Psa. 142.5

### Christ Our Passover Lamb
Clean out the old leaven so that you may be a new lump, just as you are in fact unleavened. For Christ our Passover also has been sacrificed.  1 Cor. 5.7

### The Priceless God
Yes, furthermore, I count everything as loss compared to the possession of the priceless privilege (the overwhelming preciousness, the surpassing worth, and supreme advantage) of knowing Christ Jesus my Lord *and* of progressively becoming more deeply *and* intimately acquainted with Him [of perceiving and recognizing and understanding Him more fully and clearly]. Phil. 3.8 AMP

### The Prince of Peace
Then Gideon built an altar there to the Lord and named it The Lord is Peace. Judg. 6.24

For a child will be born to us, a son will be given to us;  and the government will rest on His shoulders;  and His name will be called Wonderful Counselor, Mighty God, Eternal Father, Prince of Peace. Isa. 9.6

**The Preserving God**

In the presence of God, Who preserves alive all living things, and of Christ Jesus. 1 Tim. 6.13 AMP

O you who love the Lord, hate evil; He preserves the lives of His saints (the children of God), He delivers them out of the hand of the wicked. Psa. 97.10 AMP

O love the Lord, all you His godly ones! The Lord preserves the faithful And fully recompenses the proud doer. Psa. 31.23

**Notes**

**God The Ruler**
But you, Bethlehem, in the land of Judah, are not the least among the rulers of Judah; for out of you shall come a Ruler who will shepherd My people Israel.  Matt. 2.6

**God The Rock**
The Rock! His work is perfect, for all His ways are just.  Deut. 32.4

The LORD is my rock and my fortress and my deliverer, my God, my rock, in whom I take refuge; my shield and the horn of my salvation, my stronghold.  Psa. 18.2

From the end of the earth I call to You when my heart is faint; lead me to the rock that is higher than I.  Psa. 61.2

**The Restrained God**
But He, being compassionate, forgave their iniquity and did not destroy them; and often He restrained His anger and did not arouse all His wrath.  Psa. 78.38

**The Righteous God**
 A God of faithfulness and without injustice; Righteous and upright is He.  Deut. 32.4

**The Restoring God**
He restores my soul; He guides me in the paths of righteousness for His name's sake.  Psa. 23.3

Oh, that the salvation of Israel would come out of Zion! When God restores His captive people, let Jacob rejoice, let Israel be glad.  Psa. 53.6

**The Redeemer God**
As for me, I know that my Redeemer lives, and at the last He will take His stand on the earth.  Job 19.25

O LORD, my rock and my Redeemer.  Psa. 19.14

You, O LORD, are our Father, our Redeemer from of old is Your name.  Is. 63.16

**The God Of Revelation**
The God of our Lord Jesus Christ, the Father of glory, may give to you a spirit of wisdom and of revelation in the knowledge of Him.  Eph. 1.17

**My Refuge**
The Lord is my rock and my fortress and my deliverer; my God, my rock, in whom I take refuge, My shield and the horn of my salvation, my stronghold and my refuge. 2 Sam. 22.3

I will say to the Lord, "My refuge and my fortress, My God, in whom I trust!" Psa. 91.2

The Lord also will be a refuge and a high tower for the oppressed, a refuge and a stronghold in times of trouble (high cost, destitution, and desperation). Psa. 9.9 AMP

**The Resurrection**
Jesus said to her, "I am the resurrection and the life; he who believes in Me will live even if he dies. John 11.22

Blessed be the God and Father of our Lord Jesus Christ, who according to His great mercy has caused us to be born again to a living hope through the resurrection of Jesus Christ from the dead. 1 Pet. 3.2

But now Christ has been raised from the dead, the first fruits of those who are asleep. For since by a man *came* death, by a man also *came* the resurrection of the dead. For as in Adam all die, so also in Christ all will be made alive. 1 Cor. 15.20-22

**Notes**

# S

**The Sacrificial God**
Walk in love, just as Christ also loved you and gave Himself up for us, an offering and a sacrifice to God as a fragrant aroma.  Eph. 5.2

**Our God The Strong tower**
The name of the LORD is a strong tower; the righteous runs into it and is safe.  Prov. 18.1

**The God Who Sings Over Us**
The Lord your God is in the midst of you, a Mighty One, a Savior (Who saves)! He will rejoice over you with joy; He will rest (in silent satisfaction) and in His love He will be silent and make no mention (of past sins, or even recall them); He will exult over you with singing. Zeph. 3.17 AMP

**The Servant God**
For you first, God raised up His Servant and sent Him to bless you by turning every one of you from your wicked ways. Acts 3.26

By His knowledge the Righteous One, my Servant, will justify the many, as He will bear their iniquities.  Is. 53.11

**The Savior God**
I, even I, am the LORD, and there is no savior besides Me.  Is. 43.11

Looking for the blessed hope and the appearing of the glory of our great God and Savior, Christ Jesus.  Titus 2.13

**The Satisfying God**
Who satisfies your years with good things, so that your youth is renewed like the eagle.  Psa. 103.5

**The Strong God**
The Lord is the Strength and my (impenetrable) Shield; my heart trust in; relies on, and confidently leans on Him, and I am helped.  Psa. 28:7

The Lord is my Strength, my personal bravery, and my invincible army; He makes my feet like hind's feet and will make me able to walk and make progress upon my high places.  Hab. 3:19

The name of the LORD is a strong tower; the righteous runs into it and is safe.  Prov. 18.1

**The God Who Is Our Shield**
But You, O Lord, are a shield about me,  my glory, and the One who lifts my head. Psa. 3.3

My God, my rock, in whom I take refuge,  my shield and the horn of my salvation, my stronghold and my refuge;  my savior, You save me from violence. 2 Sam. 22.3

**Notes**

### The Triumphant God
When He had disarmed the rulers and authorities, He made a public display of them, having triumphed over them through Him.  Col. 2.15

But thanks be to God, who always leads us in triumph in Christ, and manifests through us the sweet aroma of the knowledge of Him in every place.  2 Cor. 2.14

### The God Who Is Truth
It is the Spirit who testifies, because the Spirit is the truth.  1 John 5.6

Jesus said to him, "I am the way, and the truth, and the life; no one comes to the Father but through Me."  John 14.6

O send out Your light and Your truth, let them lead me; let them bring me to Your holy hill and to Your dwelling places.  Psa. 43.3

### The Trustworthy God
The Lord is trustworthy.  1 Cor. 7.25

In the hope of eternal life, which God, who cannot lie, promised long ages ago.  Titus 1.2

### The God Who Is A Tower
The name of the LORD is a strong tower; the righteous runs into it and is safe.  Prov. 18.10

For You have been a refuge for me, a tower of strength against the enemy.  Psa. 61.3

### Notes

**The Upright God**
A God of faithfulness and without injustice, Righteous and upright is He.  Deut. 32.4

Good and upright is the LORD; Therefore He instructs sinners in the way.  Psa. 25.8

**The Unsearchable God**
Great is the LORD, and highly to be praised, and His greatness is unsearchable.  Psa. 145.3

Oh, the depth of the riches both of the wisdom and knowledge of God! How unsearchable are His judgments and unfathomable His ways!  Rom. 11.33

**The Unchanging God**
For I, the LORD, do not change; therefore you, O sons of Jacob, are not consumed.  Mal. 3.6

**The Understanding God**
With Him are wisdom and might; To Him belong counsel and understanding.  Job 12.13

The Spirit of the LORD will rest on Him, The spirit of wisdom and understanding.  Is. 11.2

**Notes**

# V

### The Victorious God
The LORD your God is in your midst, a victorious warrior.  Zeph. 3.17

And in Your majesty ride on victoriously, for the cause of truth and meekness and righteousness.  Psa. 45.4

Thanks be to God, who gives us the victory through our Lord Jesus Christ.  1 Cor. 15.57

### The Visionary God
The counsel of the LORD stands forever, the plans of His heart from generation to generation.  Psa. 33.11

"For I know the plans that I have for you," declares the LORD, "plans for welfare and not for calamity to give you a future and a hope."  Jer. 29.11

### The God Who Has A Voice
The LORD also thundered in the heavens, and the Most High uttered His voice.  Psa. 18.13

The voice of the LORD is upon the waters; the God of glory thunders, The LORD is over many waters. The voice of the LORD is powerful, the voice of the LORD is majestic.  Psa. 29.4

**Notes**

**The Winning God**
I am the first and the last, and the living One; and I was dead, and behold, I am alive forevermore, and I have the keys of death and of Hades. Rev. 1.17,18

**The Wise God**
To the only wise God, through Jesus Christ, be the glory forever. Amen. Rom. 16.27

**God The Way**
Jesus said to him, "I am the way, and the truth, and the life; no one comes to the Father but through Me." John 14.6

**The Warrior God**
The LORD will go forth like a warrior, He will arouse His zeal like a man of war. Is. 42.13

Gird Your sword on Your thigh, O Mighty One, In Your splendor and Your majesty! Psa. 45.3

He who sat on it is called Faithful and True, and in righteousness He judges and wages war. Rev. 19.11

The LORD is a warrior; The LORD is His name. Ex. 15.3

**The Wholly Desirable God**
His mouth is full of sweetness. And he is wholly desirable. This is my beloved and this is my friend, O daughters of Jerusalem. Song 5.16

**The Wise God**
To God our Savior, Who alone is wise, be glory and majesty, dominion and power, both now and forever. Amen. Jude 1:25

**Notes**

_____

_____

_____

_____

# Z

**The Zealous God**
The zeal of the Lord of hosts shall perform this.  2 Kings 19.31

His disciples remembered that it was written, "ZEAL FOR YOUR HOUSE WILL CONSUME ME."  John 2.17

Then the LORD will be zealous for His land and will have pity on His people.  Joel 2.18

**Notes**

# Who You Are To Me

The verses in this section have been adjusted intentionally so that you can read them directly to God and pray them as though they were prayers from you to Him.

## You Are The God Who Is Humble

| | |
|---|---|
| Zechariah 9.9 | Behold, [You are] coming to [us]; [You are] just and endowed with salvation, humble, and mounted on a donkey, even on a colt, the foal of a donkey. |
| Luke 22.27 | And [You] said to them…"For who is greater, the one who reclines at the table or the one who serves? Is it not the one who reclines at the table? But I am among you as the one who serves." |
| Phil. 2.6-8 | Although [You] existed in the form of God, [You] did not regard equality with God a thing to be grasped, but emptied [Yourself], taking the form of a bond-servant, and being made in the likeness of men. Being found in appearance as a man, [You] humbled [Yourself] by becoming obedient to the point of death, even death on a cross. |
| Psalm 113.2-6 | Blessed be [Your] name, [Lord], from this time forth and forever. From the rising of the sun to its setting, [Your name] is to be praised. [You are] high above all nations; [Your] glory is above the heavens. Who is like the Lord our God, who is enthroned on high, who humbles Himself to behold *the things that are* in heaven and in the earth? |
| Matt. 11.28-30 | [You said to] Come to [You], all who are weary and heavy-laden, and [You would] give [us] rest. [We should] take [Your] yoke upon [us] and learn from [you], for [You are] gentle and humble in heart and [we would] find rest for [our] souls. For [Your] yoke is easy and [Your] burden is light." |

## You Are The Coming King

Rev. 22.13      [You are] the Alpha and the Omega, the first and the last, the beginning and the end.

Rev. 1.5-7      Jesus Christ, the faithful witness, the firstborn of the dead, and the ruler of the kings of the earth. [You have loved] us and released us from our sins by [Your] blood" and [You have] made us to be a kingdom, priests to [our] God and Father—to [You] be the glory and the dominion forever and ever. Amen. Behold, [You are] coming with the clouds and every eye will see [You], even those who pierced [You]; and all the tribes of the earth will mourn over [You].

Matt. 24.30-31      And then [Your sign] will appear in the sky, and then all the tribes of the earth will mourn, and they will see [You] coming on the clouds of the sky with power and great glory. And [You] will send forth [Your] angels with a great trumpet and they will gather together [Your] elect from the four winds, from one end of the sky to the other.

Eph. 1.9-10 (NIV)      And [You] made known to us the mystery of [Your] will according to [Your] good pleasure, which [You] purposed in Christ, to be put into effect when the times will have reached their fulfillment—to bring all things in heaven and on earth [summing up of all things] together under one head, even Christ.

1 Corinthians 15.28      When all things are subjected to [You], then the Son Himself also will be subjected to the One who subjected all things to [You], so that [You] may be all in all.

John 14:1-3 (NIV)      [I will] not let [my heart] be troubled. [I] believe in God; [and I] believe also in [You]. [Your] Father's house has many rooms... [You are] going there to prepare a place for [me]. And if [You] go and prepare a place for [me], [You] will come back and take [me] to be with [you] that [I] also may be where [You are].

## You Are The God Who Has All Authority

Matthew 28.18      And [You] spoke to them, saying, "All authority has been given to Me in heaven and on earth."

Eph. 1.20-23      [Jesus, you have been raised] from the dead and seated at [The Father's] right hand in the heavenly places, far above all rule and authority and power and dominion, and every name that is named, not only in this age but also in the one to come. And [the Father has] put all things in subjection under [Your] feet, and [has given You] as head over all things.

Phil. 2.9-11      God highly exalted [You], and bestowed on [You] the name which is above every name, so that at [Your name] every knee will bow, of those who are in heaven and on earth and under the earth, and that every tongue will confess that [You are] Lord, to the glory of God the Father.

Psalm 24.1 (NIV)      The earth is [Yours], and everything in it, the world, and all who live in it.

Colossians 2.15      When [You] had disarmed the rulers and authorities, [You] made a public display of them, having triumphed over them through Him.

| | |
|---|---|
| Num. 14.20 | As [You] live, all the earth will be filled with the glory of the Lord. |
| Psalm 74.16-17 (NKJV) | The day is Yours, the night also is Yours; You have prepared the light and the sun. You have set all the borders of the earth; You have made summer and winter. |
| Psalm 75.2-3 (AMP) | When the proper time has come [for executing Your judgments], [You] will judge uprightly. When the earth totters, and all the inhabitants of it, It is [You] who will poise and keep steady its pillars. |
| Psalm 115.2-3 | Why should the nations say, "Where, now, is their God?" But our God is in the heavens; He does whatever He pleases. |
| Daniel 2.20-21 | Let [Your name] be blessed forever and ever, for wisdom and power belong to [You]. It is [You] who changes the times and the epochs; [You remove] kings and establish kings. |

## You Are The Mighty God

| | |
|---|---|
| Nah. 1.5 (NIV) | The mountains quake before [You] and the hills melt away. The earth trembles at [Your] presence, the world and all who live in it. |
| Psalm 97.1-6 (NIV) | [You reign], let the earth be glad; let the distant shores rejoice. Fire goes before [You] and consumes [Your] foes on every side. [Your] lightning lights up the world; the earth sees and trembles. The mountains melt like wax before [You], before the Lord of all the earth. The heavens proclaim [Your] righteousness, and all the peoples see [Your] glory. |
| Psalm 33.6-11 | By [Your word] the heavens were made, And by the breath of [Your] mouth all their host. [You] gather the waters of the sea together as a heap; [You] lay up the deep in storehouses. Let all the earth fear [You]; Let all the inhabitants of the world stand in awe of [You]. For [You] spoke, and it was done; [You] commanded, and it stood fast. [You nullify] the counsel of the nations; [You] frustrate the plans of the peoples. [Your counsel] stands forever, the plans of [Your] heart from generation to generation. |
| Psalm 44.2-3 | You with Your own hand drove out the nations [before Joshua]; Then You planted them [Your sons and daughters]; For by their own sword they did not possess the land, And their own arm did not save them, But Your right hand and Your arm and the light of Your presence, For You favored them. |
| Psalm 74.15-17 (NKJV) | You broke open the fountain and the flood; You dried up mighty rivers. The day is Yours, the night also is Yours; You have prepared the light and the sun. You have set all the borders of the earth. |
| Job 36.5 | Behold, [You] is mighty but [You do] not despise *any*; {You are} mighty in strength of understanding. |
| Psalm 89.7,8 | [You are a] God greatly feared in the council of the holy ones, and awesome above all those who are around [You]. O Lord God of hosts, who is like You, O mighty Lord? Your faithfulness also surrounds You. |

## You Are Glorious

Psalm 8.1 (NIV) — LORD, our Lord, how majestic is Your name in all the earth! You have set Your glory in the heavens.

Psalm 19.1-2 (NIV) — The heavens declare [Your glory]; the skies proclaim the work of [Your] hands. Day after day they pour forth speech; night after night they reveal knowledge…

Psalm 72.5-11 (NKJV) — They shall fear You as long as the sun and moon endure, throughout all generations. [You] shall come down like rain upon the grass before mowing, like showers that water the earth. In [Your] days the righteous shall flourish, and abundance of peace, until the moon is no more. [You] shall have dominion also from sea to sea, and from the river to the ends of the earth. Those who dwell in the wilderness will bow before [You], and [Your] enemies will lick the dust… All nations shall serve [You].

Psalm 86.8-10 (NKJV) — Among the gods there is none like You, O Lord; Nor are there any works like Your works. All nations whom You have made shall come and worship before You, O Lord, And shall glorify Your name. For You are great, and do wondrous things; You alone are God.

Psalm 93.1-2 (NKJV) — [You reign], [You are] clothed with majesty; [You are] clothed, [You have] girded [Yourself] with strength. Surely the world is established, so that it cannot be moved. Your throne is established from of old; You are from everlasting.

Psalm 96.6 (AMP) — Splendor and majesty are before [You], Strength and beauty are in [Your] sanctuary.

Revelation 21.23 — The city had no need of the sun or of the moon to shine in it, for [Your glory] illuminated it. [You], the Lamb [are] it's light.

Isaiah 12.4,5 (NIV) — [I will] give praise to [You] Lord, [I will] proclaim [Your] name; [I will] make known among the nations what [You have] done, and proclaim that [Your] name is exalted. [I will] sing to the Lord, for [You have] done glorious things, let this be known to all the world.

## You Are Beautiful

Psalm 45.1-2 — My heart overflows with a good theme; I address my verses to [You]; My tongue is the pen of a ready writer. You are fairer than the sons of men; Grace is poured upon Your lips; Therefore God has blessed You forever.

Isaiah 4.2 (NKJV) — In that day, [You,] the Branch of the LORD shall be beautiful and glorious;

Isaiah 9.6 (NKJV) — …And [Your] name will be called Wonderful…

Isaiah 28.5 (NIV) — In that day [You,] the Lord Almighty, will be a glorious crown, a beautiful wreath for the remnant of [Your] people.

## You Are Righteous And Just

| | |
|---|---|
| Deut. 32.3-4 (NIV) | I will proclaim [Your name]. Oh, praise the greatness of our God! [You are] the Rock, [Your] works are perfect, and all [Your] ways are just. A faithful God who does no wrong, upright and just [are You]. |
| Psalm 9.4-6 | You have sat on the throne judging righteously. You have rebuked the nations, You have destroyed the wicked; You have blotted out their name forever and ever. The enemy has come to an end in perpetual ruins, And You have uprooted the cities; The very memory of them has perished. |
| Psalm 36.6 (NIV) | Your righteousness is like the mighty mountains, Your justice like the great deep. |
| Psalm 45.3-7 | Gird Your sword on Your thigh, O Mighty One, in Your splendor and Your majesty! And in Your majesty ride on victoriously, for the cause of truth and meekness and righteousness; let Your right hand [display awesome deeds]. Your arrows are sharp; the peoples fall under You; Your arrows are in the heart of the King's enemies. Your throne, O God, is forever and ever; a scepter of uprightness is the scepter of Your kingdom. You have loved righteousness and hated wickedness. |
| Psalm 71.19 | Also Your righteousness, O God, is very high, You who have done great things; O God, who is like You? |
| Psalm 96.10,13 (AMP) | [I will] say among the nations that the Lord reigns; the world also is established, so that it cannot be moved; [You] shall judge and rule the people righteously and with justice...[You come] to judge and govern the earth! [You] shall judge the world with righteousness and justice and the peoples with faithfulness and truth. |

## You Are Happy

| | |
|---|---|
| Heb. 1.9 | God has anointed You with the oil of gladness more than Your companions. |
| Hebrews 12.2 | Jesus...for the joy set before [You, You] endured the cross, despising the shame, and [have] sat down at the right hand of the throne of God. |
| John 15.11 | These things [You] have spoken to [me] so that [Your] joy may be in [me], and that [my] joy may be made full. |

## You Are The One Who Sees and Cares

| | |
|---|---|
| Psalm 33.13-15 | [You look] from heaven; [You] see all the sons of men; from [Your] dwelling place [You] look out on all the inhabitants of the earth, [You] who fashion the hearts of them all, [You] who understands all their works. |
| Psalm 33.18 | Behold, [Your eye] is on those who fear [You], on those who hope for [Your] lovingkindness. |

| | |
|---|---|
| 2 Chronicles 16.9 | For [Your eyes] move to and fro throughout the earth that [You] may strongly support those whose heart is completely [Yours]. |
| Hebrews 4.13 | And there is no creature hidden from [Your] sight, but all things are open and laid bare to the eyes of Him with whom we have to do. |
| Psalm 34.15 | [Your eyes] are on the righteous and [Your] ears are attentive to their cry. |
| Psalm 56.8 | You have taken account of my wanderings; put my tears in Your bottle. Are they not in Your book? |

## You Are Loving And Caring

| | |
|---|---|
| Psalm 31.21 | Blessed be [You, O] LORD, for [You] have made marvelous [Your] lovingkindness to me in a besieged city. Lord, through all my troubles You have made marvelous to me Your great love. |
| Psalm 33.5 | The earth is full of [Your] lovingkindness. [You are] near to the brokenhearted and [save] those who are crushed in spirit. |
| Psalm 36.5,7-9 | Your love, O LORD, reaches to the heavens, Your faithfulness to the skies. How priceless is Your unfailing love! Both high and low among men find refuge in the shadow of Your wings. [I] feast on the abundance of Your house; You give [me] drink from Your river of delights. For with You is the fountain of life. |
| Psalm 68.19 | Blessed [are You, Lord], who daily bears [my] burden. |
| Psalm 94.18-19 (AMP) | When I said, "my foot is slipping," Your mercy and lovingkindness, O Lord, held me up. In the multitude of my [anxious] thoughts within me, Your comforts cheer and delight my soul! |
| Psalm 66.20 | Blessed be [You, O] God, [You have] not turned away [my] prayer, nor [Your] lovingkindness from [me]. |
| Psalm 103.8-17 (NKJV) | [O Lord You are] compassionate and gracious, slow to anger, abounding in love. [You do] not treat [me] as [my] sins deserve or repay [me] according to [my] iniquities. For as high as the heavens are above the earth, so great is [Your] love for those who fear [You]; as far as the east is from the west, so far [have You] removed our transgressions from us. As a father has compassion on his children, so [You O] LORD [have] compassion on those who fear [You]; for [You know] how [I am] formed, [You remember] that [I am] dust. But from everlasting to everlasting the LORD's love is with those who fear Him. |
| Psalm 145.17-20 (NKJV) | [You are] righteous in all [Your] ways, gracious in all [Your] works. [You are] near to all who call upon [You], To all who call upon [You] in truth. [You] will fulfill the desire of those who fear [You]; [You] also will hear [my] cry and save [me]. [You, O] LORD [preserve] all who love [You]. |
| John 3.16 | For [You] so loved the world that [You] gave your only son, that whoever believes in Him would not perish but have everlasting life. |

# You Are My Protector

| | |
|---|---|
| Psalm 3.1-3 | You, O LORD, are a shield about me, my glory, and the One who lifts my head. |
| Psalm 7.10 (NIV) | My shield is [You, Lord], who saves the upright in heart. |
| Psalm 28.8 | The LORD is [my] strength, and [You are] a saving defense to [Your] anointed. |
| Isa. 52.12 | For [You] will go before [me], and the God of Israel will be [my] rear guard. |
| Isa. 54.17 | No weapon that is formed against [me] will prosper; and every tongue that accuses [me] in judgment [I] will condemn. This is the heritage of the servants of the LORD, and [my] vindication is from [You]. |
| Psalm 4.8 | [I] will lie down and sleep in peace, for You alone, O LORD, make [me] dwell in safety. |
| Psalm 27.1-6 | The LORD is my light and my salvation; whom shall I fear? The LORD is the defense of my life; whom shall I dread? When evildoers came upon me to devour my flesh, my adversaries and my enemies, they stumbled and fell. Though a host encamp against me, my heart will not fear; though war arise against me, in spite of this I shall be confident. One thing I have asked from the LORD, that I shall seek: that I may dwell in the house of the LORD all the days of my life, to behold the beauty of the LORD and to meditate in His temple. For in the day of trouble [You] will conceal me in [Your] tabernacle; in the secret place of [Your] tent [You] will hide me; [You] will lift me up on a rock. And now my head will be lifted up above my enemies around me, and I will offer in [Your] tent sacrifices with shouts of joy: I will sing, yes, I will sing praises to the LORD. |
| Psalm 71.24 (NIV) | My tongue also shall talk of Your righteousness all the day long. For they are confounded, for they are brought to shame who seek my hurt. |
| Psalm 76.1-7 (NIV) | In Judah [You are] known; [Your] name is great in Israel. [You] broke the flashing arrows, the shields and the swords, the weapons of war. You are resplendent with light, more majestic than mountains rich with game. Valiant men [the pride of the enemy] lie plundered, They sleep their last sleep; not one of the warriors can lift his hands. At your rebuke, O God of Jacob, both horse and chariot lie still. You alone are to be feared. Who can stand before You when You are angry? |
| Psalm 121.5-8 (NKJV) | The LORD is [my] keeper; [You are my] shade at [my] right hand. The sun shall not strike [me] by day, Nor the moon by night. The LORD shall preserve [me] from all evil; He shall preserve [my] soul. The LORD shall preserve [my] going out and [my] coming in from this time forth, and even forevermore. |
| Psalm 27.1,2 | [Lord, You are] my light and my salvation; Whom shall I fear? [You are] the defense of my life; Whom shall I dread? |
| Psalm 23.4 | Even though I walk through the valley of the shadow of death, I fear no evil, for You are with me; Your rod and Your staff, they comfort me. |
| Psalm 41.1,2 | How blessed [am I when I] considers the helpless; The Lord will deliver [me] in a day of trouble. The Lord will protect [me] and keep [me] alive, and [I] shall be called blessed upon the earth. |

# You Are My Success

| | |
|---|---|
| Psalm 127.1-2 | Unless [You], the LORD, builds the house, [I will] labor in vain [as I] build it; Unless the LORD guards the city, The watchman keeps awake in vain. It is vain for [me] to rise up early [in toil], to retire late, to eat the bread of painful labors; for [You give to Your] beloved even in [my] sleep. |
| Psalm 18.36 | You enlarge my steps under me, and my feet have not slipped. |
| Psalm 44.4-8 | You are my King, O God; command victories for Jacob. Through You we will push back our adversaries; through Your name we will trample down those who rise up against us. For I will not trust in my bow, nor will my sword save me. But You have saved [me] from [my] adversaries and You have put to shame those who hate [me]. In God [I] have boasted all day long and [I] will give thanks to Your name forever. |
| Psalm 146.3,5 | [I] do not trust in princes, in mortal man, in whom there is no salvation. How blessed is he whose help is the God of Jacob, whose hope is in the LORD his God. |
| Psalm 108.12-13 (AMP) | Give us help against the adversary, for vain is the help of man. Through and with God we shall do valiantly, for [it is You] who shall tread down our adversaries. |
| Psalm 20.7 (NIV) | Some trust in chariots and some in horses, but [I will] trust in the name of the LORD [my] God. |
| Psalm 33.16-20 | The king is not saved by a mighty army; a warrior is not delivered by great strength. A horse is a false hope for victory; nor does it deliver anyone by its great strength. Behold, the eye of the LORD is on those who fear Him, on those who hope for His lovingkindness, to deliver his soul from death and to keep him alive in famine. [My] soul waits for the LORD; [You are my] help and [my] shield. |
| Psalm 37.1-5 | [I] do not fret because of evildoers, [I will] be not envious toward wrongdoers. For they will wither quickly like the grass and fade like the green herb. [I will] trust in the LORD and do good; [I will] dwell in the land and cultivate faithfulness. [I] delight [myself] in the LORD; And [You] will give [me] the desires of [my] heart. [I] commit [my] way to the LORD, trust also in [You], and [You] will do it. |
| Psalm 121.1-3 | [I] will lift up [my] eyes to the hills— from whence comes [my] help? [My] help comes from the LORD, who made heaven and earth. [You] will not allow [my] foot to be moved; [You] who keeps [me] will not slumber. |
| Psalm 62.1,5-7 | [My] soul waits in silence for God only; from [You] is [my] salvation. [My] soul, wait in silence for God only, for [my] hope is from [You]. [You] only [are my] rock and [my] salvation, [my] stronghold; [I] shall not be shaken. On God [my] salvation and [my] glory rest; the rock of my strength, [my] refuge is in God. |

## You Are God My Provider

Psalm 17.14 (NIV)    You still the hunger of those you cherish; their sons have plenty, and they store up wealth for their children.

Psalm 105.37,39-41,44 (NIV)    [You] brought out Israel [from Egypt], laden with silver and gold, and from among their tribes no one faltered... [You] spread out a cloud as a covering, And a fire to give light at night. They asked, and [You] brought them quail and satisfied them with the bread of heaven. [You] opened the rock, and water gushed out; like a river it flowed in the desert. [You] gave them the lands of the nations, and they fell heir to what others had toiled for.

Proverbs 13.21-22    [You said], the righteous will be rewarded with prosperity... and the wealth of the sinner is stored up for the righteous.

Psalm 66.12    You made men ride over our heads; We went through fire and through water, Yet You brought us out into a place of abundance.

Psalm 112.1-10    Praise the LORD! How blessed is the man who fears the LORD, who greatly delights in [Your] commandments. [My] descendants will be mighty on earth; the generation of the upright will be blessed. Wealth and riches are in [my] house, And [my] righteousness endures forever. Light arises in the darkness for the upright; [I am] gracious and compassionate and righteous. It is well with the man who is gracious and lends; [I] will maintain [my] cause in judgment. For he will never be shaken; the righteous will be remembered forever. [I] will not fear evil tidings; [my] heart is steadfast, trusting in the LORD. [My] heart is upheld, [I] will not fear, Until [I] look with satisfaction on [my] adversaries.

Matt 6.30-33    But if [You], God, so clothes the grass of the field, which is alive today and tomorrow is thrown into the furnace, will [You] not much more clothe [me]? ...[I will not] worry then, saying, 'What will [I] eat?' or 'What will [I] drink?' or 'What will [I] wear for clothing?' For the Gentiles eagerly seek all these things; for [my] heavenly Father knows that [I] need all these things. But [if I] seek first [Your] kingdom and [Your] righteousness, all these things will be added to [me].

Phil. 4.19    And [You] will supply all [my] needs according to [Your] riches in glory in Christ Jesus.

## You Are My Guide

Proverbs 16.9 (NKJV)    [My] heart plans [my] way, But [You O] LORD [direct my] steps.

Psalm 23.3 (NKJV)    [You lead] me in the paths of righteousness For [Your] name's sake.

Psalm 37.23-24 (NKJV)    The steps of a good man are ordered by the LORD, And [You delight] in [my] way. Though [I] fall, [I] shall not be utterly cast down; For [You O LORD uphold me] with [Your] hand.

Psalm 73.23-24 (NKJV)    [I am] continually with You; You hold [me] by [my] right hand. You will guide [me] with Your counsel, And afterward receive [me] to glory.

| | |
|---|---|
| Isaiah 30.19-21 (NIV) | [I] will weep no more. How gracious [You are] when [I] cry for help! As soon as [You hear], [You] will answer [me]. Although [You give me] the bread of adversity and the water of affliction, [my] teachers will be hidden no more; with [my] own eyes [I] will see them. Whether [I] turn to the right or to the left, [my] ears will hear a voice behind [me], saying, "This is the way; walk in it." |

## You Are The God Who Answers Prayer

| | |
|---|---|
| Psalm 102.17 (NKJV) | [You] will respond to the prayer of the destitute; [You] will not despise their plea. |
| James 5.16 (AMP) | [You said that] the earnest (heartfelt, continued) prayer of a righteous man makes tremendous power available [dynamic in its working]. |
| John 16.23-24 | [Jesus, You said], Truly…if [I] ask the Father for anything in [Your] name, He will give it to [me]….ask and [I] will receive, so that [my] joy may be made full. |
| 1 John 3.21-22 (AMP) | [I] have confidence (complete assurance and boldness) before God, and [I] receive from Him whatever [I] ask, because [I] [watchfully] obey His orders [observe His suggestions and injunctions, follow His plan for [me]] *and* [habitually] practice what is pleasing to Him. |
| Mark 11.22-24 | [You told us] "Have faith in God. [that] whoever says to this mountain, 'Be taken up and cast into the sea,' and does not doubt in his heart, but believes that what he says is going to happen, it will be granted him. [You said],"Therefore…, all things for which you pray and ask, believe that you have received them, and they will be granted you. |
| Luke 11.9-13 (AMP) | {Jesus, You said to me], ask and keep on asking and it shall be given [me]; seek and keep on seeking and [I] shall find; knock and keep on knocking and the door shall be opened to [me]. For everyone who asks and keeps on asking receives; and he who seeks and keeps on seeking finds; and to him who knocks and keeps on knocking, the door shall be opened. {You told me], what father among you, if his son asks for a loaf of bread, will give him a stone; or if he asks for a fish, will instead of a fish give him a serpent? Or if he asks for an egg, will give him a scorpion? If [I] then, evil as {I am], know how to give good gifts to [my] children, how much more will [my] heavenly Father give the Holy Spirit to those who ask and continue to ask Him! |

## You Are My Rest

| | |
|---|---|
| Psalm 37.3-5 (AMP) | [I will] trust (lean on, rely on, and be confident) in the Lord and do good; so shall [I] dwell in the land and feed surely on His faithfulness, *and* truly [I] shall be fed. [If I] delight [myself] also in the Lord, and [You] will give [me] the desires *and* secret petitions of [my] heart. [If I] commit [my] way to the Lord [roll and repose each care of [my] load on [You]]; trust (lean on, rely on, and be confident) also in Him and He will bring it to pass. |
| Psalm 38.15 | For [I] hope [wait with expectation] in You, O LORD; You will answer, O Lord my God. |

| | |
|---|---|
| Psalm 127.2 (NKJV) | It is vain for [me] to rise up early [in toil], To retire late, To eat the bread of painful labors; For [You give to Your] beloved even in [their] sleep. |
| Psalm 132.1-2 | O LORD, [my heart is] not proud, nor [my] eyes haughty; Nor do [I] involve [myself] in great matters, or in things too difficult for [me]. Surely [I] have composed and quieted [my soul]; like a weaned child rests against its mother, [my soul is] like a weaned child within [me]. |
| Psalm 116.7 (NKJV) | Return to your rest, O my soul, For the LORD has dealt bountifully with you. |
| Psalm 23.1-3 | [You are] my shepherd, I shall not want. [You make] me lie down in green pastures; [You lead] me beside quiet waters. [You restore] my soul; [You guide] me in the paths of righteousness For [Your] name's sake. |

## You Are The God Who Is For Me

| | |
|---|---|
| Psalm 18.19 | [I say like David said], [You] brought me forth also into a broad place; [You] rescued me, because [You] delighted in me. |
| Psalm 56.9 | This I know, that God is for me. |
| Psalm 118.6-7 | The LORD is for [me]; [I] will not fear; What can man do to [me]? The Lord is for [me] among those who help [me]. |

## You Are My Portion

| | |
|---|---|
| Gen 15.1 (NKJV) | [You are my] shield, [my] exceedingly great reward. |
| Psalm 119.57 (NKJV) | You are my portion, O LORD. |
| Psalm 73.25-26 (AMP) | Whom have I in heaven but You? And I have no delight *or* desire on earth besides You. My flesh and my heart may fail, but God is the Rock *and* firm Strength of my heart and my Portion forever. |

## You Are My Sustainer

| | |
|---|---|
| Psalm 3.5 | I lay down and slept; I awoke, for the LORD sustains me. |
| Psalm 54.4 | Behold, God, [You are] my helper; The Lord is the sustainer of my soul. |
| Psalm 55.22 | [I] cast [my] burden upon [You O] LORD and [You] will sustain [me]; [You] will never allow the righteous to be shaken. |

# Proclamation Prayer

# What is Proclamation Prayer?

All of us have been deceived. The enemy has sown lies into our lives and as a result, unbelief abounds. What do we *really* believe about God? We know that God is able to, but because of difficult circumstances, life experience and just plain human nature, we are not sure if He will do it for us.

"God, I know that You *can,* but *will* You do it for me?"

This lie is the oldest weapon the enemy has. It is the original deception. If the enemy can convince you to question God's faithfulness, He can also lead to you into countless areas of sin and error. But we have been given divine power to tear down the lies we believe about God. The weapon that we have been given to overcome the lies and see our circumstances change is the truth. When we begin to declare that truth out of our mouths, things begin to change.

Proclamation prayer is simply declaring what God says about Himself over whatever circumstance, problem or crisis that you may face. It is very similar to adoration prayer but where adoration prayer is a language of love, proclamation prayer is the language of war. It is stepping into your God-given authority to speak to the issues and see them move.

James the apostle said this about prayer: "The earnest (heartfelt, continued) prayer of a righteous man makes tremendous power available [dynamic in its working]." James 5.16 (AMP)

When we pray in agreement with God's truth, we enter into a dynamic and powerful relationship with God's word that has the ability to accomplish great things.

**Proclamation prayer does three things:**

1. **Transforms your mind** – Our minds are one of the keys to the change we seek. Our minds are transformed by the Word of God as we begin to speak it out.

2. **Stirs up faith to believe** - It is not enough that we know the word; we have to allow it to penetrate into our inner being and stir up faith. Without faith, we cannot please God and the way to faith is by speaking out what God has done and is doing for us right now.

3. **Activates the power of God** – As you begin to proclaim the nature of God, the natural world begins to respond. Your circumstances begin to change; your future begins to look different. Your whole life begins to be aligned with the purpose of God. Proclamation activates the power of God over circumstances because we are aligning our hearts with God's will by declaring His nature.

**Proclamation Prayer: The Simple Steps.**

1. Ask yourself these questions: What issues or circumstance am I facing right now? Do these circumstances line up with who God is? You now have a target for your proclamation prayers.

2. Take the adoration scriptures or the pre-written prayers and begin to declare the nature of God that is related to the circumstance you face. Using the scripture keeps us aligned with the nature of God and the truth of what He says about Himself.

3. As you begin to pray, pray from a place of authority. Remember who you are as the child of God and an heir of the King. You have the authority to ask and know that you will be heard.

The next few pages are examples of Proclamation prayer that you can use to get you started on the journey. You can also use the names of God from the Adoration section of this manual and turn them into Proclamation prayers.

For a more in-depth teaching on Proclamation prayer, check out "You Shall Know The Truth" by Ben Woodward. You can purchase it from www.benwoodward.com.

# God The Provider

## A proclamation of God as a provider

Father, I bless You today as I begin to declare who You are. There has never been anyone who has cared for me like You have. You have watched over me with such unrelenting love. When I think about the ways You have led me, I cannot help but be amazed at the way You love me. I want to thank You for always loving me. I confess over my own life that I am Your child and You are my Father. Because of this, I have complete access to You and the riches of Your storehouse today.

### You Provide As A Shepherd

I declare that You are God my provider. Your word tells me in *Psalm 23* that You are my shepherd and I shall not want. I declare that when my will is aligned to Your will, there can never be a time when I am in want. You are leading me like a shepherd leads his sheep and I shall never lack any good thing. I will not push back against Your leadership because I know that when I walk with You I find my true purpose. I find my identity, health, peace and fullness in You. Your word tells me that if I "seek first [Your] kingdom and [Your] righteousness, all these things will be added to [me]."[2] I declare over my life that I will set Your kingdom as my one pursuit. I will set all my energy and life in finding and gaining You and Your kingdom. I know that as I do this You will never leave me lacking. You always ensure that my needs will be met. The Psalmist said, "I have never seen the righteous forsaken, or his descendants begging bread."[3] I declare this promise over my family, my children and my future generations. We will not be those begging bread but we will be those who will have more than enough and we will be a supplier for the sake of others. Just as Joseph, in the midst of the

---

[2] Matt. 6.33
[3] Psalm 37.25

famine had a storeouse, I will have a storehouse that is full and available to be able to feed others and give to those in need. Father God, make me a blessing to others by filling my cup to full and overflowing. This is my inheritance as Your child. Jesus never lacked for a thing while He was on the earth. He told me never to worry about food or clothing. He said the birds of the air are cared for by You. How much more can I trust You as my provider and as my shepherd?

## You Provide Just In Time

I declare the same words Abraham spoke about You in the book of Genesis. "Abraham called the name of that place The LORD Will Provide."[4] You are my provider. You are the source of all that I need for my life. I know that at times I have tried to make You do things in my timing and not Yours. As a result, I have birthed Ishmaels that have been a source of pain for my family and me. Today I declare that my future will not be determined by the poor choices I have made in my past. Today I choose what is right. I will say like Joshua did as he stood before the children of Israel, "...as for me and my house, we will serve the Lord."[5] This is the day that changes everything. This is the day when my future is before me and I have the strength to lay hold of it. I declare that You will provide for me all that You said You would. You are "not slow about [Your] promise, as some count slowness, but [You are] patient toward [me]."[6] You will accomplish all that You promised and at just the right time, You will answer the promise of my youth. You will answer release my inheritance and will provide all that You promised because You are my provider. You are faithful to fulfill all that You promised in me by providing all that You said You would, just in time. I declare today that I will trust You with the timing but at the same time, I will do all that I can to hasten the day by declaring Your nature. I know Your nature and that provokes me to declare your nature over my future, my family and my inheritance. You are the provider for my family, my business, my vocation and my future. Provide all that I will need to accomplish all that You have called me to accomplish in the days ahead.

## You Provide A Better Way Than My Way

I declare that as my provider I can trust You when You ask me to lay certain things down in my life. I know that it is always better for me to obey than to hold on to that which I think is the pathway to my inheritance. Just like You asked Abraham to sacrifice Isaac, I proclaim today that I will be faithful to say yes when You ask me to lay down those things that have been a source of supply for me. I know that You truly are my provider, not the tools You have given me. In all the areas of my life I will learn to say that You are the Lord who Provides. If my health is in question, I will say that You are the Lord who Provides for my health. If my finances are in question, I will say that You are the Lord who Provides my finances. If my family circumstances are in question, I will say that You are the Lord who Provides stability in my family. I will go up to the mountain of the Lord and I will say yes to the way You lead my life. I will lay my most valuable promises on the altar because none are as valuable as the knowledge of You as my provider. I will choose,

---

[4] Genesis 22.14
[5] Josh. 24.15
[6] 2 Pet. 3.9

just as Abraham did, to make a covenant with You by leaning into Your ability to provide and remember that this is not just a nice idea - this is Your name. I declare You over my life as the God who provides for me.

## You Provide Overflowing Blessing

Just as You declared in Psalm 23 that we shall not want, You also say in Your word that "[You] will supply all [my] needs according to [Your] riches in glory in Christ Jesus."[7] What great and wonderful promises You have for us in Your word. I am determined to not take a single one for granted. I will stand upon every promise You made toward me. I know that not one single word will ever fail because Your word will not return void[8]. Today, I stare into the glory of the riches of Christ Jesus and I think upon the fullness of what that means for me. I declare that You said You would "open for [me] the windows of heaven and pour out for [me] a blessing until it overflows."[9] Today I receive of that fullness of blessing, not out of vanity or a desire to be rich but out of a desire to receive from a good Father. I declare that You want to give these things to me. You own the cattle on every hill and the wealth of every mine. My needs are not so great that You cannot fill them and still have an abundance to spare. I declare today that I have come to sit at Your banqueting table and partake of all the riches You have for me. I will no longer listen to the lies that have kept me from being bold enough to ask more of You.

## You Provide Because You Have Overcome

I reject the lie that I cannot trust Your provision because of my past failures. I reject the lie that I cannot trust Your provision because of my circumstances. I reject the lie that my provision comes from my abilities, my knowledge, my intellect, or even my physical capacity in any way. I come to declare You as my sole provider and source of success. I declare today that my provision comes as a direct result of the death and resurrection of Jesus. Because He lives and He has overcome, I am provided for. Because He sits at the right hand of the Father, my provision is secured. I am a co-heir with Christ and a partaker of the divine nature. Today I renew my covenant of mercy with You and I stand beneath the covering that You have provided for me as part of my sonship. I declare that You are my provider. Thank You that You hear every word that has been spoken and are acting on my behalf, even as I speak.

---

[7] Phil. 4.19
[8] Isa. 55:11
[9] Mal. 3:10

# God The Healer

## A proclamation of God as the Healer

Father, I declare today that You are Jehovah Rapha, the God who heals. Thank You that it is not only written in Your word, but the proof of Your healing power has been demonstrated throughout history as men and women who were afflicted were raised up and set free from the curse of sickness and death. What an amazing gift it is to know and to walk in the knowledge of Your nature as the God who heals. Thank You that You are directing this attribute of Yourself toward me today as I pray.

### Your Death Provides My Healing

Today, I declare the truth spoken about Jesus as it is written in the book of Isaiah, "But He was pierced through for our transgressions, He was crushed for our iniquities, the chastening for our well-being fell upon Him, and by His scourging [stripes, wounds] we are healed."[10] Father, I stand before You to remember the price that was paid for my healing. I think about the blood that was shed by Your Son as He willingly went to the cross on my behalf. He did it not only for the saving of my soul but the redemption of my body. Father, is there anyone like You in all the earth? There is no one else. You made a way for the curse of sickness to be lifted off my body. You revealed Your glory by declaring it to the prophet Isaiah hundreds of years before it became apparent in the life of Jesus. It was always in Your character to be the great physician of our souls. Not only did You make provision for our eternal wellbeing but You also made a way for our bodies to walk in fullness all the days of our life. You declared Your own name as the God who heals in the book of Exodus when You said, "If you will give earnest heed to the voice of the LORD your God, and do what is right in His sight, and give ear to His commandments, and keep all His statutes, I will put none of the diseases on you which I have put on the Egyptians; for I, the LORD, am your healer."[11] Father, today I can stand in confidence knowing that You are who You say You are. You do not change and just as You were the healer to the

---

[10] Isaiah 53.5
[11] Exodus 15:26

children of Israel thousands of years ago, You are our healer today. I declare that this is Your name and today I am standing upon Your name for my healing. The apostle Peter also spoke of Your character as the healer in First Peter when he said, "He Himself (Jesus) bore our sins in His body on the cross, so that we might die to sin and live to righteousness; for by His wounds you were healed."[12]

## My Healing Is A Legal Right

Father, I stand before You and I remind You of the blood that was shed by Your Son Jesus for my healing. I petition heaven right now for the release of that which is my divine inheritance. I declare that it is no longer okay to watch as the very healing that is a spiritually legal right for my life is not present in my flesh. Father, I ask that You would look again upon the Son that sits at Your right hand in the place of authority and judgment and remember the scars that He bears in His body for my sickness. Father, look upon the scars and respond to that witness in heaven by releasing Your healing power upon the earth today. This sickness and disease that remains in the lives of those I love stands in opposition to Your established order and kingdom. The apostle John testified of Jesus that, "The Son of God appeared for this purpose, to destroy the works of the devil."[13] Father, today I respond to Your word and stand before You to declare Your nature again. Not only is it in Your character to heal but also, by the death and resurrection of Your Son, You made a way for that healing to be made available in my life. The book of Romans tells me that, "if the Spirit of Him who raised Jesus from the dead dwells in [me], He who raised Christ Jesus from the dead will also give life to [my] mortal bod[y] through His Spirit who dwells in [me]."[14] Father, I declare that it is Your Spirit working in me that raises me up and sets my feet upon a solid rock. I will declare Your nature and receive healing for my mortal body today.

## You Renew My Strength

Today, I come into agreement with the psalmist as he wrote in the Psalms, "Bless the LORD, O my soul, and forget none of His benefits; who pardons all your iniquities, who heals all your diseases; who redeems your life from the pit, who crowns you with lovingkindness and compassion; who satisfies your years with good things, so that your youth is renewed like the eagle."[15] What great promises You have for me today as I believe You for my healing. I declare that You are the God who satisfies my years with good things and restores my body to health. I will not respond by what I see with my eyes or what I hear with my ears; I will respond to Your nature as the God who loves me, is for me, and is my healer. God, I declare that I will forget none of Your benefits today. I am determined to go back and remember all the good that You have done for me in the years gone by. I want thankfulness to be the testimony of my life as I continue to believe You for my health and the health of my loved ones. I declare that the goodness of God has been my shield all the days of my life. No matter what the circumstances may look like in front of me, I know that my God is good. I will declare Your goodness toward me regardless of the circumstances. I will not allow the lie of my condition or

---

[12] 1 Peter 2.24
[13] 1 John 3.8
[14] Romans 8.11
[15] Psalm 103.2-5

my circumstances to tell me who You are, I will stare into the knowledge of You and be transformed into Your image day by day. I declare what Isaiah says about You in the book of Isaiah, "Do you not know? Have you not heard? The Everlasting God, the LORD, the Creator of the ends of the earth does not become weary or tired. His understanding is inscrutable. He gives strength to the weary and to him who lacks might He increases power. Though youths grow weary and tired, and vigorous young men stumble badly, Yet those who wait for the LORD will gain new strength, they will mount up with wings like eagles, they will run and not get tired, they will walk and not become weary."[16]

## You Cast Down All Lies

Father, today I declare that I will not give the devil any credit for his lies. I will simply declare what the book of Isaiah says over my life, "No weapon that is formed against [me] will prosper, and every tongue that accuses [me] in judgment [I] will condemn. This is the heritage of the servants of the LORD, and their vindication is from [the LORD]."[17] My vindication is coming from the Lord God and Him alone. It is the answer to the injustice that is occurring due to sickness and disease. The price for true healing has already been paid. I declare that there is not a weapon that has been formed against me that can do any harm. I speak to every accusation that tells me that this sickness is a result of my sin in any way or a result of my family history or my family genetics. I declare that Jesus' blood is enough to redeem me from all of my past, present, and future mistakes, all of my family's history, and that from this moment on I break every agreement with the lies I have believed. I will no longer carry the burden of feeling like I have to earn my healing. I plead the blood of Jesus and say that His blood is enough. I will declare over my life what is revealed in the book of Colossians, "For [God] rescued us from the domain of darkness, and transferred us to the kingdom of His beloved Son."[18] As a citizen of the Kingdom of Jesus, I am no longer subject to the laws and decrees of the kingdom of this world and I take a stand against the lie that says that I am to remain bound to sin, sickness, and disease.

Father, I declare today that You are my strength and hope in times of trouble. I declare that I can lean into You when it seems like all else has failed and trust in Your ability to carry me through the storms that momentarily pass me by. I will declare about You as it says in First John, "This is the confidence which we have before Him, that, if we ask anything according to His will, He hears us. And if we know that He hears us in whatever we ask, we know that we have the requests which we have asked from Him."[19] Father, I lean into You as the Healer today, knowing that You hear me as I pray and are moving on my behalf even at this moment.

---

[16] Isaiah 40.28-31
[17] Isaiah 54.17
[18] Colossians 1.13
[19] 1 John 5.14-15

# The Pure God

## A proclamation of God as pure

Lord, today I come to You to proclaim Your nature as the pure God. It is my heart's desire to become pure as You are pure and to become holy as You are holy. I know one of the most effective ways to become like You is to stare into who You are. Today I come to stare into Your purity. I come to gaze into Your heart that burns with a passion for my purity and declare Your nature as the pure God.

### I Am Pure Because You Are Pure

Father, I declare Your nature as the pure God as it is written in First John, "Beloved, now we are children of God, and it has not appeared as yet what we will be. We know that when He appears, we will be like Him, because we will see Him just as He is. And everyone who has this hope fixed on Him purifies himself, just as He is pure."[20] Your purity is the example of how I should live as Your child. You call me Your child and just as You give me the hope of becoming like You, You also call me to the place of purity by using Yourself as the example of the purity I am supposed to pursue. Father, I know I have no hope of becoming pure without Your help, but I love that You call me to this standard of purity. Thank You that in this verse You have given me the way to enter into purity. You say that it is by seeing You as You are. Father, I declare You as the pure God and declare that Your purity makes me fall in love with You even more. Your purity causes me to realize how much You sacrificed when You gave Your Son for me.

---

[20] 1 John 3.2-3

## I Am Pure Because I Am Your Body

Father, You are the pure God. All of scripture points to Your purity and to the holiness that defines You. I declare what is written in the book of Daniel, "I kept looking until thrones were set up, and the Ancient of Days took His seat; His vesture was like white snow and the hair of His head like pure wool. His throne was ablaze with flames, its wheels were a burning fire."[21] Father, You are clothed in garments that are white as snow. There is not a blemish in anything that You are clothed in. I love that Your word tells me that Jesus also is clothed in garments of white. I know that because I am a part of the body of Christ, pure white clothing also clothes me. I declare that because You are pure and because Your garments are white, that means that I, as Your body, am also clothed in pure white. You are not just covering over Your blemished body; You are purifying me and counting me worthy of being a part of Your body. Father, I declare that because You are pure, Jesus is pure and because Jesus is pure, then I am pure.

## You Make A Way For Me To Be Pure

Father, I thank You that because of Your purity, You hate sin. I know You especially hate sin because of how it cripples me and hinders me from becoming all that You want me to be. In Your hatred for sin, You made a way for it to be destroyed in me. Thank You that You do not just forgive my sin, You have a passionate desire to deliver me from it in the future. Thank You for the prayer Jesus prayed and taught the disciples to pray, "And do not lead us into temptation, But deliver us from evil."[22] Thank You that Jesus knew temptation was going to be a reality so He gave us an example of how to overcome, and it is by looking to You, our Father in heaven. So, I look to You and stare into the face of purity. I declare that You are the God who will lead me not into temptation but will deliver me from evil. Father, I thank You for what Jesus said in the book of Matthew, "Blessed are the pure in heart, for they shall see God."[23] I declare what You said in the book of Ezekiel, "I will sprinkle clean water on you, and you will be clean; I will cleanse you from all your filthiness and from all your idols. Moreover, I will give you a new heart and put a new spirit within you; and I will remove the heart of stone from your flesh and give you a heart of flesh."[24] You are the pure God and You are making us pure because You are making us into Your image. I declare that I no longer have a heart of stone that cannot respond to You. I have a heart of flesh that is able to listen, to respond, and to change when You speak to me. I declare that You have cleansed me with water and washed away all my filthiness. I declare that all this is a result of who You are as the pure God.

## Purity Brings Friendship

I speak out the truth which is found in the book of Proverbs, "He who loves purity of heart and whose speech is gracious, the king is his friend."[25] Lord, it is my heart's desire to be Your friend and to know You. I see that

---

[21] Daniel 7.9
[22] Matt.6.13
[23] Matthew 5.8
[24] Ezekiel 36.26
[25] Proverbs 22.11

the entrance to the place of friendship with You is to love purity. Today, I make it my passionate pursuit to become pure as You are pure. I want to enter into that level of friendship. I know my heart is often deceived and turns to wickedness but I also know that if I continue to declare You as the pure God and I set my heart to love purity, You will meet me where I am. You remind me of how You don't just love me because You have to, You actually like me because You want to. You want me to be Your friend and You are committed to my purity and to sustaining me in the pressure of the day to day temptations. You are passionate about making me pure. Today, I declare that You are the pure God and I will be pure just as You are pure.

## Purity Brings Joy

Lord, as I seek You to discover who You are as the pure God, I declare a releasing of joy in my life which comes from true purity. I declare that joy is a natural by-product of true purity and this is why You are the happiest person in the universe. The book of Psalms says this about You, "You have loved righteousness and hated wickedness; Therefore God, Your God, has anointed You with the oil of joy above Your fellows."[26] Because of Your purity and Your love of righteousness, You have been given the capacity for more joy than any other. I declare that as I enter into purity with You, You will also release to me "joy inexpressible and full of glory".[27] If purity brings true joy, then I want to be more like You and be pure as You are pure. You are the example of how real purity produces real joy. I know the world has tried to convince me that joy comes from doing what I want, whenever I want. I confess that many times I have believed that lie and have tried to find joy in sin and unrighteousness. It is true that there was temporary pleasure, but I declare that there was no true joy. I know that I have fed my flesh on too many occasions in the hope that it would lead me to happiness. I know that as I seek the pure God, I will become pure as You are and as a result You will fill me with true pleasure and true joy that does not fade but lasts forever. I bless You as the Pure God today and thank You for Your transforming power that makes me pure as I stare into Your purity.

---

[26] Psalm 45.7
[27] 1 Pet. 1.8

# The God Who Is For Me

## A proclamation of God as the "for me" God

Father, I run to You today as I seek to discover the truth about the "God who is for me." When I think about my life, I realize that most of it has been spent running from You rather than running to You. I realize that I have not seen You as a God who is concerned about my needs or my heart. I have only ever seen You as a God who is waiting for me to make a mistake so that You can punish me. I have spent most of my life trying to give You as little time as possible because I thought You were not happy about being with me. Today, I come to see You as the God who is passionately for me and who loves to see my success in life.

### You Are 'For Me' With Compassion

Father, I declare today the very words that Jesus spoke when He was describing the kind of father that You are. He said in the story about the prodigal son, "But when he was yet a great way off, his father saw him, and had compassion, and ran, and fell on his neck, and kissed him."[28] Father, Your heart is so full of compassion toward me. Even when I am a great way off because of the poor decisions I have made, You have those eyes that burn with a flame of fire for me. You see me even at my weakest point and still You say about me that I "have ravished [Your] heart with one glance of [my] eye."[29] Who would run into the arms of a son who had wasted the family fortune? You are so completely for me that You will overlook my failures to reach me and let me know how much You love me. Father, I declare today that You are the God who is for me in such a way that You will run to meet me. I know that I have pictured You as stoic and unemotional, but You are far from that. You may sit in the heavens as King of Kings but You are also the Father who runs to meet His sons and daughters in need. You have such a plan for me and You are so full of compassion when I fail to walk in the path You have placed before me. You love me and are for me, even still today.

---

[28] Luke 15.20
[29] Song 4:9 NKJV

## You Have A Plan For Me

I declare what You said through the prophet Jeremiah, "For I know the plans that I have for you,' declares the LORD, 'plans for welfare and not for calamity to give you a future and a hope."[30] Father, I know that these are not just idle words spoken years ago to another generation. You have a great plan for my future and even now You are working to see it accomplished. Your plan cannot fail when it comes to me because You are the God who has never failed in anything You have set out to do. When I commit my ways to the Lord, there is not a thing that could stand in the way of Your will and Your plan for my life being fulfilled. I know at times it seems like things may have been delayed, but I will yet declare You as the God who is for me. You are fully aware of the plans You have for me and I am confident that not one thing has been forgotten. You will accomplish what You said You would by giving me a future and a hope. Thank You that You are restoring hope to me today by reminding me that You have not forgotten me. You have not forgotten any of the promises You made to me concerning my life. Every time I feel myself getting into despair I just remember your name. When I remember Your word, I am set ablaze again to declare You as the God who is for me. You have a plan for me. You have a future for me. You have a desire that I would live all my days grounded in hope because of who You are. I remember all the things that You have done in the past for me. The way You have loved me, the way You have provided for me and the way You have planted my feet on the Rock that is your son Jesus. I will not let my circumstances dictate my belief about how You feel about me; I will let Your word remind me of the way that You are for me.

## You Are My Success

Father, I declare the words that Jesus spoke in the book of Matthew, "and who of you by being worried can add a single hour to his life?"[31] How much time and energy have I wasted by not seeing You as the God who is for me? I have worried about my life far too much and this day I make my declaration that I will no longer live a life of worry. I will live a life of trusting in the God who is for me. I declare that all that I am is Yours, so I give You permission to do with me as You see best. You know exactly how I was made and You know exactly what I need to fulfill my purpose in this life. I declare that because You are the God who is for me, I cannot fail in what I am called to do. I have only one option, and that is to succeed. I want to see my life differently today; I want to see it through the eyes of the God who is for my success. I know that this does not always mean an easy or comfortable life, but it does mean that I can trust it will be the best life possible. I am confident that no matter what happens, You are working behind the scenes to ensure my success.

---

[30] Jer. 29.11
[31] Matt. 6.27

## You Delight In Me

I proclaim today the same words that King David wrote in the Psalms when he was delivered from his enemies, "[You] brought me forth also into a broad place; [You] rescued me, because [You] delighted in me."[32] Father, I declare that You are the God who takes me from my narrow view of who You are to a broad place where I can fully understand who You are. I confess that my understanding of You has been limited by my experience in this life. But You are not limited by my lack of understanding! You know my weak frame and that is why You are so determined to rescue me and set me in a broad place. You are on a mission to radically transform the way I think about You. Once You have done that, You will enable me to see myself rightly through Your eyes. Father, what an incredible thing it is to know that You delight in me. I know that this delight does not come from what I do for You but who I am to You. You are the God who is for me and delights in me today and all the days of my life. You may be sad over my sin at times, but You always delight in me as a child.

## You Came To Save Me

Father I declare that the greatest thing You did to prove how much You are for me was to send Your son, Jesus. I declare what Jesus said in the book of John, that "[You] so loved the world, that [You] gave [Your] only begotten Son, that whoever believes in Him shall not perish, but have eternal life. For [You] did not send the Son into the world to judge the world, but that the world might be saved through Him."[33] Father, I know that so many times I have heard this verse and overlooked the power of what it means to me. But today I stare into the truth of Your word and declare that You loved me with such a great love that You ransacked heaven on my behalf and sent Your Son to save me. You said that You did not come to condemn us but to save us. So Father, I proclaim today that You are for me, far more than I could have ever dreamed was possible. You proved it by sending Your very own son into the world to ensure that not only am I saved eternally, but I am also given the chance to enter into the perfect will of God for my life today. Father, I believe in Your son. I believe that You are for me and I believe that You have loved me with an everlasting love. I declare what Jesus also said in the book of John, "that [I] may be perfected in unity, so that the world may know that You sent [Jesus], and loved [me], even as You have loved [Jesus]."[34] Father, I proclaim that You love me with the same measure that You love Jesus! How could I ever doubt that You are for me? How can I ever again doubt whether or not You have my future in the palm of Your hands? Did Jesus ever doubt Your love? He never once doubted whether or not You were for Him and just as You were for Jesus, so You are for me.

Father, I will not doubt You any longer, I will believe that You are for me no matter what the circumstances say. No matter what happens in the earth, in my life, or in my family, I know that You are the God who is for me. Today, I stand upon the truth that God is for me.

---

[32] Psa. 18.19
[33] John 3.16-17
[34] John 17.23

# The King of Kings

A proclamation of God as King of kings

Lord, I come to You with a thankful heart this day, recognizing that You have loved me and made a way for me to have access to your throne room right now. I thank You for the blood of Your Son that gave me access to You. I thank You for the power of Your Holy Spirit that enables me day by day to walk in the knowledge of You. I thank You for Your mercy toward me as my Father, and ask that You would speak to me concerning Your kingdom and the work of Your kingdom today.

## You Are King Of Kings And Lord Of Lords

Father I proclaim today the words of the book of Revelation, "and on His robe and on His thigh He has a name written, '"KING OF KINGS, AND LORD OF LORDS'."[35] I proclaim this day to the earth and to the heavens that there is one King who rules over the affairs of all things. I declare that there is one King who raises up men and tears them down and one King who establishes order and justice in the earth. His kingdom will know no end and His glory will know no bounds. His majesty and His power will be proclaimed in all the nations of the earth and He will rule in justice and peace forever over the kingdoms of the earth. I declare today that "Your throne, O God, will last forever and ever; a scepter of justice will be the scepter of Your kingdom."[36] Your throne has existed from time past and will continue to the end of the ages. Though men may rule over us for a moment, only God can establish their place. Thank You, Father, that You are in control of the nations and there is not a devil or a man who can move You from Your throne. The kings of the earth may try to take a stand against You, but He who sits in the heavens laughs at them.[37] It is only because of Your mercy that they endure and only because of Your righteous justice that they are removed. The leadership of the heavens and the earth are in Your hands. I declare that these same hands that lead the earth and the nations are the same hands that carry my heart and my future. I am completely overwhelmed

---

[35] Revelation 19.16
[36] Psa. 45.6 NIV
[37] Psa. 2.2-4

that the King of Kings has taken such a great interest in my life and my future, but I stand in thankfulness for this reality today.

## I Will Willingly Call You King

I declare today that, "The bird also has found a house, and the swallow a nest for herself, where she may lay her young, even Your altars, O LORD of hosts, my King and my God."[38] Lord God, I declare that You are King over my life this day. If the birds of the field can find a place at Your courts, how much more can Your son find a place in Your court? I proclaim that Your kingdom is at work in my life today and it is a kingdom of righteousness and peace. Even as the book of Isaiah says that "there will be no end to the increase of His government or of peace,"[39] I proclaim that Your government is a government of peace to those who love You. Today, I declare that Your government will be at work in my life to bring forth peace for my heart. You are at work today revealing the places where my life is in opposition to Your kingdom. Where there are lies which stand in opposition to Your rule and strongholds that have been built in opposition to Your leadership, You are coming to tear them down. I recognize that while these things remain, there can be no peace in my life. Father, I ask You for the continued work of Your Holy Spirit to bring forth Your kingdom in my life today. Tear down every high thing, "Every lofty thing raised up against the knowledge of God, and [take] every thought captive to the obedience of Christ."[40] Father, I declare that I will willingly subject my life to Your leadership as King of Kings and will willingly allow the work of Your kingdom in my life. I proclaim that as a result, "The King will desire [my] beauty. Because He is [my] Lord, [I will] bow down to Him."[41]

## You Are King Over The Problems In The Earth

Father, I trust in Your perfect justice as King over the nations. I proclaim what Jeremiah said about You, "But the LORD is the true God; He is the living God and the everlasting King. At His wrath the earth quakes, and the nations cannot endure His indignation."[42] You are the true God and the everlasting King. Where other kings manifest themselves for a moment, You last forever. The Psalms declare that "The LORD sat as King at the flood; yes, the LORD sits as King forever."[43] No matter what happens in the earth, though it be floods, earthquakes, wars, famine or plague, You sit in the place of leadership over the nations. You are the Chief Commander over the nations of the earth and not one thing happens without Your knowing. Because You are in control, I can perfectly trust Your leadership over the earth. Even when I don't understand it, I can lean into Your faithfulness as the eternal, true, wise and just King. I will declare what Isaiah said about You, "For the LORD is our judge, the LORD is our lawgiver, the LORD is our king; He will save us."[44] You, My King and My God, You will save us. Lord, it is true that at times what I see in the earth can be terrifying and upsetting. Sometimes I do not understand, but even when I don't understand I will continue to declare my trust in Your

---

[38] Psalm 84.3
[39] Isaiah 9.7
[40] 2 Cor 10:5
[41] Psalm 45.11
[42] Jer. 10.10
[43] Psalm 29.10
[44] Is. 33.22

leadership over the nations. I can trust You when the earth quakes because I know Your heart of compassion for the nations and that "It is not the will of [my] Father who is in heaven that one of these little ones perish." If this is Your heart, and You are the eternal King, then I can trust Your wisdom in knowing the end from the beginning. I am also confident that just like Moses did, I can plead for mercy on behalf of those You love, knowing that You will hear my voice and will relent concerning the things that are coming to the earth. [45]

## You Are King Over My Family

Jesus, I declare You as King over my family today. Just as Joshua declared over His family before the children of Israel, so I will declare over my family today, "But as for me and my house, we will serve the LORD."[46] I desire to have no king over my house but Jesus. I admit that there have been many things that have tried to rule my house, including the love of money, entertainment, comfort and the love of 'things.' Today, I proclaim that the only law that I will lead my family by is the law of love. Father, I desire that at the center of my family we would place Your throne and Your ways. I thank You that as I place my family under Your leadership, we now bear the mark of being children of the King and all that comes with being a part of Your royal family. We are no longer our own; we are the Lord's and He is able to lead us and guide us as He sees fit. This means that no matter what happens I will always declare over my family, "He is the blessed and only Sovereign, the King of kings and Lord of lords."[47]

## Your Leadership Is Perfect

Father, I remember again today Your leadership as King of Kings. I recall how You have led the nations through history and how Your perfect leadership has always been seen when the day breaks and the shadows flee away. I declare that even in the midst of the darkest night I can trust Your perfect leadership as King of Kings. There is no night so dark that You cannot peer into it because, "even the darkness is not dark to You, and the night is as bright as the day. Darkness and light are alike to You."[48] Thank You that today You are King over every circumstance, every trial, every hardship, every glory, every triumph and every success. Thank You, Jesus, for Your eternal glory as King of Kings and Lord of Lords.

---

[45] Matt. 18.14
[46] Josh. 24.15
[47] 1 Tim 6.15
[48] Psa. 139.12

# God The Protector

## A proclamation of God as a protector

Blessed is the Lord God Almighty who is my protector and my hope all the days of my life. Thank You that as I come today to proclaim Your nature as a protector, I will begin to see Your nature revealed in every area of my life. When I look at the world, I find myself getting into fear about the future, but today I remember what the Apostle Peter said about You, that I should "[cast] all [my] anxiety on [You], because [You care] for [me]."[49] This is my hope. Whatever my concern or fear is today, I can trust that You are able to take care of it. I proclaim over my life that God is more than enough for any circumstance. My hope is in Jesus today. He is the King of Kings and Lord of Lords and He is my protector every day.

### Perfect Love Casts Out Fear

Lord, I thank You for what the psalmist said about You, "The LORD will protect [me] and keep [me] alive, and [I] shall be called blessed upon the earth."[50] Lord, I thank You that no matter what danger I face, I can trust the hand of the Lord because You are my protector. You are my Father and my safety is in Your hands. Just like a baby trusts the safety of a mother's arms, so I can trust You. I can lean into Your chest and hear Your heart as it beats for me. Lord, so many times I get into unbelief because of fear and as a result, I try to find ways to protect myself. I want to be totally dependant upon You! My own ways have failed so many times but You have never failed me. You have always been faithful. "Perfect love casts out fear,"[51] and because You are perfect love, I can let go of all my fears and lean into You. As I do, Your promise is that I shall be called blessed upon the earth. People are going to look at me and see how I live in complete trust and call me blessed. Thank You that You are my protector today and always.

---

[49] 1 Pet. 5.7
[50] Psalm 41.2
[51] 1 John 4.18

## Your Eye Is Always On Me

Thank You Lord that You not only keep me in the midst of physical danger but you also deliver me from spiritual danger. The Psalms declare that, "The LORD will protect [me] from all evil; He will keep [my] soul."[52] I know that I have an enemy who seeks to kill, steal, and destroy. But I thank You Lord that You are far stronger than any enemy that might face my soul. When I am faced with temptation, You always "provide the way of escape also, so that [I] will be able to endure it."[53] My soul can be at peace whenever I am faced with a spiritual trial because in the midst of the trial, You are my Protector. I proclaim today that You are the God who, "supports the fatherless and the widow."[54] Your eye is constantly on those who are oppressed and in need. Even when it seems like my needs are small, You care. You are always watching over me and You really do see even the small things. You are responding to Your nature as the Faithful God when you protect us just as Paul wrote, "But the Lord is faithful, and He will strengthen and protect you from the evil one."[55] I proclaim Your faithfulness today as the reason for my protection. It is not because of anything I have earned or anything I have done; it is simply because of who You are.

## My Psalm 91 Protector

I will declare what the psalmist spoke about my protection in Psalm 91, "[As I dwell] in the shelter of the Most High [I] will abide in the shadow of the Almighty. I will say to the LORD, 'My refuge and my fortress, My God, in whom I trust.' For [You deliver me] from the snare of the trapper and from the deadly pestilence. [You] will cover [me] with [Your] pinions, and under [Your] wings [I will] seek refuge; [Your] faithfulness is a shield and bulwark. [I] will not be afraid of the terror by night, or of the arrow that flies by day; of the pestilence that stalks in darkness, or of the destruction that lays waste at noon. A thousand may fall at [my] side and ten thousand at [my] right hand, but it shall not approach [me]. [I] will only look on with [my] eyes and see the recompense of the wicked. For [I] have made the LORD, my refuge, even the Most High, [my] dwelling place. No evil will befall [me], nor will any plague come near [my] tent. For He will give His angels charge concerning [me], to guard [me] in all [my] ways. They will bear [me] up in their hands, that [I] do not strike [my] foot against a stone. [I] will tread upon the lion and cobra, the young lion and the serpent [I] will trample down. 'Because he has loved Me, therefore I will deliver him; I will set him securely on high, because he has known My name. He will call upon Me, and I will answer him; I will be with him in trouble; I will rescue him and honor him. With a long life I will satisfy him and let him see My salvation [says the Lord].'"

Father, thank You for all the promises that are in this Psalm. I proclaim today that You are my refuge and my fortress and in You, I really do trust. I trust that You are able to be my shield no matter what comes my way. I trust that You love me and have a plan for me. I proclaim today that your protection extends to my physical body as well as my spiritual person. I declare that sickness and disease shall not come near me because God is my protector. I declare that because the angels of God have been charged with my protection, I can trust that they are fully able to accomplish the will of God toward me. I declare that I do love You and because I love You, You will answer my call and satisfy me all the days of my life. I proclaim today that through faith in

---
[52] Psalm 121.7
[53] 1 Cor. 10.13
[54] Psa. 146.9
[55] 2 Th. 3.3

God and who He is, I am established. I declare what Peter said, "[We] are protected by the power of God through faith for a salvation ready to be revealed in the last time." [56] I will be set in a high place and I will be protected until the end because I trust not in anything that man can do for me, but, "In God, whose word I praise, in God I have put my trust; I shall not be afraid. What can mere man do to me?"[57]

## No More Fear About The Future

Father, today I put my trust You as my protector. When I hear noises in the night and my heart leaps within me, I will put my trust in You. When I look at my children and wonder what will happen to them, when I wonder if they will make good choices or not, I will proclaim You as their protector. When I think about the future and all that is to come and how You told me that, "In the world you have tribulation," I will trust you. I confess that it makes me fearful at times but I will not be ruled by fear. You went on to say, "but take courage; I have overcome the world."[58] You were so confident and I take hold of that confidence today. I will stand confidently and declare "Behold, God is my salvation, I will trust and not be afraid; For the LORD GOD is my strength and song, and He has become my salvation."[59] I declare that whatever plan the enemy has had to bring me down will fail. I speak confusion into every plan and every work the enemy has designed against me and declare, "No weapon that is formed against [me] will prosper; and every tongue that accuses [me] in judgment [I] will condemn."[60] This is my inheritance as a child of the living God and I lay hold of it today. I declare You as my protector.

Thank You that today I can put my trust in You and know that "Indeed, none of those who wait for You will be ashamed."[61]

---

[56] 1 Pet. 1.5
[57] Psa. 56.4
[58] John 16.33
[59] Is. 12.2
[60] Is. 54.17
[61] Psa. 25.3

# A Life Of Faith

## A proclamation of a life of faith out of Hebrews 11

Father, thank you for all of the mercy you have shown me. Thank you for showering Your love upon me. There has never been a moment when You did not think of me with the utmost care and concern. There was never a moment when You did not offer me everything I need for life and godliness.[62] You have called me to Yourself and it is not by might I come, nor in the strength of my own arms or the wisdom of my own mind. I come in the power of the Holy Spirit[63] and because of Jesus shed blood, I have access to Your throne room of grace. Your word tells me in the book of Hebrews that faith is the substance of things hoped for, the evidence of things unseen.[64] Your word goes on to describe the miracle of faith as it activated supernatural power in the lives of normal men and women throughout history. Today, I have come to declare that faith over my life and renew the covenant You have with me which is activated through faith. I have come because I believe that this same faith is available for a normal person like me to believe for the impossible.

### I Will Be Free From Fear

I confess that I will be a person of faith. It is my inheritance to be full of faith all the days of my life. I will no longer live in the fear of the moment or out of the fear of failure. In faith, I will believe that You are who You say You are and You are able to keep me from falling and present me blameless before You at Your appearing.[65] I recognize that in the book of Romans, Paul tells me that I am to operate according to the law of the spirit of life in Christ Jesus and not according to the law of the spirit of death.[66] I see that fear is the catalyst that binds me to death but faith sets me free to live according to the law of life in Christ Jesus. I recognize the power that fear has had in my life in the past but I say from this moment on, it will have no more power over me. It was faith that enabled Peter to get out of the boat when all the other disciples stayed because of fear. Today, I will be like Peter and step out of the boat of my past failures and mistakes and

---

[62] 2 Pet. 1.3
[63] Zech. 4.6
[64] Hebrews 11:1
[65] 1 Cor. 1.8
[66] Romans 8.2

believe that You are able to do exceedingly abundantly more in me and through me[67] because I chose to believe You. I will be a person of faith and will live only according to the law of life. I will launch out on a course that ends in a collision with heaven in my life.

## You Are The God Of The Impossible

I proclaim that You are the God who makes something out of nothing.[68] You always take the broken, discarded chaos that exists in my life and turn it into something beautiful. I believe Your word in the book of Hebrews which says, "By faith we understand that the worlds were framed by the word of God, so that the things which are seen were not made of things which are visible."[69] Today, I declare Your word over my life, and I say that You are framing my future, restoring my hope, and empowering me to believe that You are the God of the impossible. I know that through faith, every broken thing, every discarded promise and every lost dream will be restored. I confess that in the past I have carried unbelief in my life. I have allowed unbelief to be an acceptable sin within me and have let it take hold, creating strongholds of bitterness and cynicism. I will not allow unbelief in my life anymore. I will have faith in God and will be a person known for my confidence in the power of God to accomplish the impossible. I will make war against the unbelief in my soul and will no longer just passively allow it to find a place in my life, as though it has a legal right to my mind. Today, I make a stand against unbelief as I step into my inheritance as a person of faith.

## You Are The Finisher Of My Faith

You are the God who fulfills every promise You spoke to me. You are the Alpha and Omega, the beginning and the end, the first and the last. What You began in me, You will complete because You are not just the author, but also the finisher of my faith.[70] I will stir up my faith to believe that You will accomplish all You set out to do in me and believe that not one seed that has been sown in my life will be wasted. I declare that it will be for me just as it says about Sarah, "By faith Sarah herself also received strength to conceive seed, and she bore a child when she was past the age, because she judged Him faithful who had promised."[71] Father, I confess that I will have the kind of faith that enables me to bear fruit even in the place of my barrenness. Even though time and the natural order of things may stand against me, I will bear fruit in my barrenness. I speak to the seed that has been planted in the past and declare that this is the day you begin to spring up out of the ground and bring forth a harvest. I look into my past and see the seeds I have sown in people, finances, my marriage, my vocation, the church, all the places that I have scattered seed over the years. Even though the ground looks barren, behold the rain of the Holy Spirit is falling upon you and you will bring forth a harvest. Just as the desert carries dormant seeds under the soil until the time of the rain, there will yet be a harvest from the places I have sown. I speak to the seed that has not yet come forth and I say to you that you have life within you and you must bear fruit. I may have given up in times past but today, just like Sarah, I

---

[67] Eph. 3.20
[68] Gen. 1.2
[69] Hebrews 11.3
[70] Heb. 12.2
[71] Hebrews 11.11

will have faith in the God who fulfills His promises and accomplishes all that He has set out to do in me and through me.

## You are Faithful

I proclaim that I will have faith in Your unfailing love toward me. I know in times past I have doubted Your love and faithfulness even when You have proven yourself time and time again. But I look back at my own history and declare that I will view my past no longer through the lens of rejection, but through the lens of Your faithfulness and love toward me. I recognize that the enemy has tried to steal the fruit of joy in my life by causing me to believe the lies concerning Your goodness. Today, I break my agreement with the lies I have believed about You and put on faith to believe that You are who You say You are. I believe what Your word says about You and I'll have faith in the goodness of God as a generous Father toward me. I confess over my life the fruit of faith knowing that, "without faith it is impossible to please Him, for he who comes to God must believe that He is, and that He is a rewarder of those who diligently seek Him."[72] In my life today, I will live full of faith and stand ready to receive the reward You have for those who diligently seek You. I will know You as the God who "is", that You are who You say You are and You will do what You say You will do. When You say You love me, I will believe it and I will not let the lie of my circumstances, my past, or my perceived condition change the truth; I will stir up my faith to believe that I am what You say I am.

## I Will Have Faith To Believe For The Impossible

I proclaim that I will have faith in Your unchanging nature as the immutable God. I believe that what You began in me You will finish. I will also believe the testimony of all those who have gone before me. I refuse to be cynical about the work of God in my own life or in the lives of others. I will believe and respond to the testimony of others who have gone before me. I can no longer read through Your word and see the history of men and women of faith and believe it was for another person or another time. What You have done for others, You can and will do for me. When I hear a story of some individual's miraculous healing, I will apply my faith to believe that You can also use me to lay hands on the sick and see them recover. When I hear a story of a financial miracle, a relational miracle or any testimony related to the goodness of God, I will stir up my faith to believe that You can use me in the same way You have used others. I will no longer listen to the lie that God only uses special people to do special things. I will remember what the book of James has to say about Elijah: "Elijah was a man with a nature like ours, and he prayed earnestly that it would not rain; and it did not rain on the land for three years and six months. And he prayed again, and the heaven gave rain, and the earth produced its fruit."[73] What You did for Elijah, You can and will do through me. Today, I stand before You and renew my covenant of faith with You.

I will be a person with the kind of faith that moves mountains, subdues kingdoms, works righteousness, obtains promises, stops the mouths of lions, quenches the violence of fire, and escapes the edge of the sword.

---

[72] Heb. 11.6
[73] James 5.17-18

I will be one that out of weakness I am made strong. I will have the kind of faith that heals the sick, walks on water, multiplies bread and even raises the dead. I know that this is my inheritance and understanding that without faith it is impossible to please You, I take up my shield of faith out of the desire of a son to please a good Father. Thank You that You always hear my prayer and even at this moment are moving on my behalf to fulfill all that has been spoken.

# A Life Of Sonship

## A proclamation of my place as a Son of the Father

Father God, what a privilege it is to truly call You Father. The book of Romans tells me that I "have not received a spirit of slavery leading to fear again, but [I] have received a spirit of adoption as [a son] by which [I] cry out, 'Abba! Father!'"[74] Father, today I confess that You are my Abba Father and I am Your son. I confess that in the past I have viewed You through the lens of what earthly fathers have been like to me. I have responded to the title of Father as though You were distant, uncaring, abusive and many other attributes that earthly fathers have had at times. But You are not like that! Today I come to proclaim Your nature as a true Father, the perfect example of what a good Father is. I break my agreements with any lies I have believed about You as an imperfect Father. I confess You as Abba, daddy God, the Father who loves me and is for me. I know that the ability to say this does not come from my own spirit, but from the Spirit of Jesus who dwells in me. I proclaim what the book of Galatians says, "Because you are sons, God has sent forth the Spirit of His Son into our hearts, crying, 'Abba! Father!'"[75] Thank you that Your spirit is enabling me day by day to recognize and accept the truth of who You are as my Father and who I am as Your son. I am Your son and nothing can take that away.

### I Am Your Son

Father, I confess over my life what the apostle John declared. "See how great a love the Father has bestowed on us, that we would be called children of God; and such we are."[76] What kind of love is this that I should be called Your son? What a gift this is to know that I am not an orphan or a stranger in Your kingdom. I am not a servant or a slave; I am Your son. I confess over my life that I have been adopted into the family of God by the power of the Holy Spirit. I never have to be concerned about my place anymore because it is not dependent upon what I do for You, but who I am to You. Even when I have strayed in times past, You have always been waiting for me like a good Father. Instead of my shame, You gave me double honor. Instead of my filthy rags,

---

[74] Romans 8.15
[75] Galatians 4.6
[76] 1 John 3.1

You gave me garments of righteousness. Instead of my hopelessness, You gave me the hope of Your calling in my life and my inheritance as a son of the King. In the place of my barrenness, You have given me abundance. In the place of my hunger, You have set a feast before me and invited me to eat. In the place of my wanderings, You have given me a home with Yourself as a son of the King. I confess that being Your son is the greatest gift that anyone could ever receive and I receive it gladly today.

## You Love Me As A Good Father Should

I confess that, "every good thing given and every perfect gift is from above, coming down from the Father of lights, with whom there is no variation or shifting shadow."[77] Father, You do not change and I know that every gift I have ever received and every perfect thing has come from You. You are the source of every good thing that has ever come into my life because You love to give Your children good things. You love to shower upon us Your affection as a Father. Our own earthly fathers carried failure and accusations in them and responded to us out of brokenness but You carry no such thing in You. You are perfect in every way and the good things You give to me come from a heart that is not in any way trying to manipulate me. You act toward me with such kindness and even in a time of correction I can lean into Your kindness and understand that You work all things together for my good.[78] I confess that as a son, there are times when I need some correction and discipline and I will not run from it. I will welcome it because I know You are working in me to produce the image of Your Son, Jesus. I am so happy to be led by Your kindness and to become more like Jesus. I confess that day-by-day I am growing into His image and becoming more and more like a true son of the Kingdom. I confess that I will be a true son and will make war against the enemies of my soul to daily become more like You.

## I Will Be Conformed To The Image Of Jesus

I confess the words of Jesus over my life from the book of John, "that they may all be one; even as You, Father, are in Me and I in You, that they also may be in Us, so that the world may believe that You sent Me."[79] Lord, it is my ever-increasing desire to be more like You. Just as Jesus prayed, so I will also pray. I proclaim that I will labor to conform my soul to the image of Jesus and be counted worthy of becoming joined with the Father. I recognize that Jesus never did a single thing on His own; He only did what He saw His Father doing.[80] Today I will live in the same way. I will live by staring into what the Father is doing and respond to what I see. I will take the time to ask the right questions and hear from the heart of the Father before I make decisions for my life, my family, and my future. Today, I make a change regarding how I live my life. I will live walking in the footsteps of Jesus. Just as He lived, so I also will live. I will put my ear to the courts of heaven to hear what the Father is saying. I will set my eyes upon the courts of heaven to see what the Father is doing and then I will

---

[77] James 1.17
[78] Rom. 8.28
[79] John 17.21
[80] John 5.19

live my life in response to what I see and hear. I confess that this is the pathway of a true son and I will declare "yet not my will, but Yours be done."[81]

## I Am His Workmanship

I confess that I am clay in Your hands and I desire to be molded by You into whatever You would have me be. I confess that in the past I have tried to become great through my own efforts. I have tried to manipulate my future to make something of myself and by myself, just as the prodigal son did when he left with the Father's inheritance. I have gone out to make a name for myself and had not seen that all along You had a plan for me. If I just had a little more patience, I would have seen that what You had planned was far greater than I could ever dream. I confess that I have wasted my inheritance. I have squandered my right to being a son by trying to live out of my own initiative and sense of identity instead of trusting in what You had for me as a good Father. Today I confess over my life what the scriptures say in Isaiah, "But now, O LORD, You are our Father, we are the clay, and You our potter; and all of us are the work of Your hand."[82] I proclaim over my life that I am Your workmanship, created in Christ Jesus for good works, which God prepared beforehand so that I would walk in them.[83] Lord, You have prepared the good works that I am to do as a son beforehand and all I have to do is walk in them. I don't have to strive my way in. Father, I proclaim that I am Your son, You are my Father, and I will walk in Your ways today.

## I Am A Co-Heir With Christ

As Your son, I know that I have a good inheritance[84] which is secure not because of what I have done for You, but because I am a son. I confess what the apostle Paul said in the book of Romans about my place as a child. He said that "The Spirit Himself testifies with our spirit that we are children of God, and if children, heirs also, heirs of God and fellow heirs with Christ, if indeed we suffer with Him so that we may also be glorified with Him."[85] If I am a son, then my inheritance comes from my Father and I can be certain of His desire to give it to me, for, "He who did not spare His own Son, but delivered Him over for us all, how will He not also with Him freely give us all things?"[86] It is my proclamation today that I am Your son and You are my Father. It is my confession that all that I am comes from You and I will lean into Your goodness as a good Father and trust You with all of my future, my family, and my future. I thank You that even now You are pouring out the Spirit of Your Son into me and conforming me into His image so that I may become a true son of a good Father.

---

[81] Luke 22.42
[82] Isaiah 64.8
[83] Eph. 2.10
[84] Psa. 16.6
[85] Romans 8.16,17
[86] Rom. 8.32

# Who I Am To You

## I Am A Person Of Faith

1 Pet. 1.7   The proof of your faith, being more precious than gold which is perishable, even though tested by fire, may be found to result in praise and glory and honor at the revelation of Jesus Christ.

Rom. 1.17   For in it the righteousness of God is revealed from faith to faith; as it is written, "But the righteous man shall live by faith."

Gal. 2.20   "I have been crucified with Christ; and it is no longer I who live, but Christ lives in me; and the life which I now live in the flesh I live by faith in the Son of God, who loved me and gave Himself up for me.

## I Am A Person Of Power

2 Tim. 1.7   For God has not given us a spirit of timidity, but of power and love and discipline.

Col. 1.11   Strengthened with all power, according to His glorious might, for the attaining of all steadfastness and patience; joyously.

Rom. 8.11   But if the Spirit of Him who raised Jesus from the dead dwells in you, He who raised Christ Jesus from the dead will also give life to your mortal bodies through His Spirit who dwells in you.

## I Am Loved By God

| | |
|---|---|
| John 3.16 | For God so loved the world that He gave His only begotten Son, that whoever believes in Him shall not perish, but have eternal life. |
| John 16.27 | For the Father Himself loves you, because you have loved Me and have believed that I came forth from the Father. |
| 1 John 4.19 | We love, because He first loved us. |
| 1 Thess. 1:4. | We know, brothers and sisters loved by God, that he has chosen you. |

## I Am A Son

| | |
|---|---|
| Rev. 21.7 | He who overcomes will inherit these things, and I will be his God and he will be My son. |
| 1 John 3.1 | See how great a love the Father has bestowed on us, that we would be called children of God; and such we are. For this reason the world does not know us, because it did not know Him. |
| Gal. 4.7 | So you are no longer a slave but a son, and if you are a son, then you are also an heir through God. |

## I Am A Priest Of The Most High God

| | |
|---|---|
| 1 Pet. 2.9 | But you are a chosen race, a royal priesthood, a holy nation, a people for God's own possession, so that you may proclaim the excellencies of Him who has called you out of darkness into His marvelous light. |
| Rev. 1.6 | He has made us to be a kingdom, priests to His God and Father—to Him be the glory and the dominion forever and ever. Amen. |

## I Am Taken Care Of

| | |
|---|---|
| Phil. 4.19 | And my God will supply all your needs according to His riches in glory in Christ Jesus. |
| Matt. 6.30 | But if God so clothes the grass of the field, which is alive today and tomorrow is thrown into the furnace, will He not much more clothe you? You of little faith! |
| 1 Cor. 10.13 | No temptation has overtaken you but such as is common to man; and God is faithful, who will not allow you to be tempted beyond what you are able, but with the temptation will provide the way of escape also, so that you will be able to endure it. |

## I Am Valuable To God

Luke 12.24　Consider the ravens, for they neither sow nor reap; they have no storeroom nor barn, and yet God feeds them; how much more valuable you are than the birds!

Job 10.12　You have granted me life and lovingkindness; And Your care has preserved my spirit.

## I Am A Child Of God

John 1.12　But to all who have received Him--those who believe in His name--He has given the right to become God's children.

Gal. 4.7　So you are no longer a slave but a son, and if you are a son, then you are also an heir through God.

## I Am A Friend Of Jesus

John 15.15　I no longer call you slaves, because the slave does not understand what his master is doing. But I have called you friends, because I have revealed to you everything I heard from my Father.

Song 5.16　"This is my beloved and this is my friend, O daughters of Jerusalem."

## I Am No Longer A Slave To Sin

Rom 6.6　We know that our old man was crucified with Him so that the body of sin would no longer dominate us, so that we would no longer be enslaved to sin.

Rom. 8.2　For the law of the life-giving Spirit in Christ Jesus has set you free from the law of sin and death.

Gal. 5.1　For freedom Christ has set us free. Stand firm, then, and do not be subject again to the yoke of slavery.

Gal. 4.7　So you are no longer a slave but a son, and if you are a son, then you are also an heir through God.

1 Cor. 1.30　[We are in] Christ Jesus, who became for us wisdom from God, and righteousness and sanctification and redemption.

## My Body Is A Temple Of The Holy Spirit

1 Cor. 6.19　Do you not know that you are God's temple and that God's Spirit lives in you?

## I Have Been Redeemed

Rom. 3. 24   But they are justified freely by His grace through the redemption that is in Christ Jesus.

Gal. 3.13   Christ redeemed us from the curse of the Law, having become a curse for us.

Eph. 1.7   In Him we have redemption through His blood, the forgiveness of our trespasses, according to the riches of His grace.

## I Am A New Creature In Christ

2 Cor. 5.17   So then, if anyone is in Christ, he is a new creation; what is old has passed away--look, what is new has come.

Eph. 1.4   For He chose us in Christ before the foundation of the world that we may be holy and unblemished in His sight in love.

Eph. 2.4-5   But God, being rich in mercy, because of His great love with which He loved us, even though we were dead in transgressions, made us alive together with Christ--by grace you are saved.

## I Am Blessed

Eph. 1.3   Blessed is the God and Father of our Lord Jesus Christ, who has blessed us with every spiritual blessing in the heavenly realms in Christ.

Psa. 84.12   How blessed is the man who trusts in You!

Gal. 3.9   So then those who are of faith are blessed with Abraham, the believer.

Jer. 17.7   Blessed is the man who trusts in the LORD and whose trust is the LORD.

## I Am Victorious

1 Cor 15.57   But thanks be to God, who gives us the victory through our Lord Jesus Christ.

Rev. 21.11   And they overcame him because of the blood of the Lamb and because of the word of their testimony, and they did not love their life even when faced with death.

## I Am A Citizen Of Heaven

Ph. 3.20　　For our citizenship is in heaven, from which also we eagerly wait for a Savior, the Lord Jesus Christ.

1 John 2.15　　Do not love the world nor the things in the world. If anyone loves the world, the love of the Father is not in him.

## I Am Free From Sin & Sickness

1 Pet. 2.24　　And He Himself bore our sins in His body on the cross, so that we might die to sin and live to righteousness; for by His wounds you were healed.

Rom. 8.2　　For the law of the Spirit of life in Christ Jesus has set you free from the law of sin and of death.

James 5.16　　Therefore, confess your sins to one another, and pray for one another so that you may be healed. The effective prayer of a righteous man can accomplish much.

## I Am An Overcomer

1 John 5.4　　For whatever is born of God overcomes the world; and this is the victory that has overcome the world—our faith.

1 John 4.4　　You are from God, little children, and have overcome them; because greater is He who is in you than he who is in the world.

Rev. 12.11　　And they overcame him because of the blood of the Lamb and because of the word of their testimony, and they did not love their life even when faced with death.

## I Am Protected

Psa. 91.2　　He who dwells in the shelter of the Most High will abide in the shadow of the Almighty. I will say to the LORD, "My refuge and my fortress, my God, in whom I trust!"

Psa. 41.2　　The LORD will protect him and keep him alive, and he shall be called blessed upon the earth.

2 Th. 3.3　　But the Lord is faithful, and He will strengthen and protect you from the evil one.

## I Am Made In The Image Of God

Eph. 4.24　　Put on the new man who has been created in God's image--in righteousness and holiness that comes from truth.

Col 3.4　　When Christ (who is your life) appears, then you too will be revealed in glory with Him.

## I Am Your Delight

Psa. 149.4　　For the Lord takes pleasure in His people; He will beautify the afflicted ones with salvation.

Psa. 147.10-11　　He does not delight in the strength of the horse; He does not take pleasure in the legs of a man. The Lord favors those who fear Him, Those who wait for His lovingkindness.

Psa. 149.2-4　　Let Israel be glad in his Maker; Let the sons of Zion rejoice in their King. Let them praise His name with dancing; Let them sing praises to Him with timbrel and lyre. For the Lord takes pleasure in His people; He will beautify the afflicted ones with salvation.

Isa. 5.7　　For the vineyard of the Lord of hosts is the house of Israel And the men of Judah His delightful plant.

## I Am Made Righteous

2 Cor 5:21 NIV　　God made him who had no sin to be sin for us, so that in him we might become the righteousness of God.

Isa. 61.10 NIV　　I delight greatly in the Lord; my soul rejoices in my God. For he has clothed me with garments of salvation and arrayed me in a robe of his righteousness, as a bridegroom adorns his head like a priest, and as a bride adorns herself with her jewels.

Rom. 6.18 NIV　　You have been set free from sin and have become slaves to righteousness.

# More Resources

### You Shall Know The Truth
*The Power Of Adoration And Proclamation Prayer*

**Ben Woodward**

What if prayer was more than just a means to an end? What if was about encountering a living, vibrant, hopeful God?

**Your prayer life is meant to be more than just an afterthought or a boring repetitious discipline that you have to fulfill. It should be a place of dynamic encounters with truth that lead you into the knowledge of God.**

It's time for a change.

Discover the forgotten prayer tools of Adoration and Proclamation prayer and find in them the power to move mountains and change the course of your future.

Discover the Truth and let it change your life.

*Available on Amazon and at www.benwoodward.com*

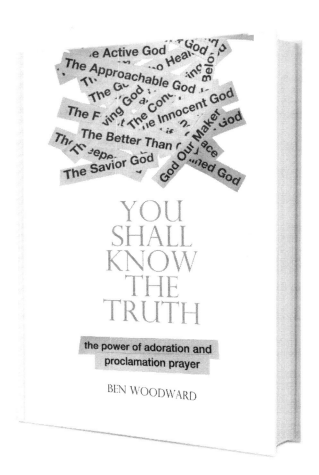

### Proclamations Volume 1 – Audio CD

This audio CD are the proclamation prayers found in this book set to music. You can purchase the Mp3's and order physical copies by going to *www.benwoodward.com*

# Discography

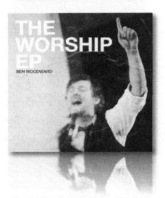

You Never Let Go – Live at The Rock of Roseville (2015)

One Voice, One Piano – Worship and Prayer (2014)

This Beautiful Life (2014)

The Worship EP (2012)

Maranatha (2010)

How We Love You (2007)

*These albums are available at www.benwoodward.com or at most online music stores.*

## Adoration App – find it on iTunes

## IRON BELL MINISTRIES
*restoring lives… unlocking destinies*

Iron Bell Ministries equips God's people to bring His kingdom to all areas of life by living out their God-given destiny. Based in Louisville, Kentucky, our heart is to help people cultivate an intimate relationship with God that allows them to partner with Him to daily live out their unique purpose. Our ministry centers on "3 Keys" the Lord has given us to see people restored and launched into their destiny.

**"The 3 Keys" to unlock life to the full:**
- *Intimacy*: Learn how to cultivate intimacy through a lifestyle of adoration prayer. Gain a healed view of who God is and a healed view of who you are in Christ.
- *Purpose*: Discover your unique destiny & how to bring God's kingdom wherever you go
- *Partnership:* Walk out your destiny daily by listening to God's voice

## Connect with us:

**Worship Nights:** Join us for corporate worship nights. We focus on adoring the Lord, equipping believers and personal ministry time.

**Iron Bell Music:** Go on the journey of discovering God's character and adoring Him in worship. Connect with our worship music from the Iron Bell barn: IRONBELLMUSIC.COM

**Equipping Events:** Several times a year we offer workshops designed to take you deeper in areas such as Adoration Prayer, our "3 Keys" to walk into your destiny, and Marriage.

**Wednesday Morning Prayer:** Join us every Wednesday morning between 7-10am at the Iron Bell for personal devotional time. There is live worship music and it's simply a time to soak in God's presence. Drop in for a few minutes or for several hours.

For more information, or to be added to our mailing list, visit our website: IronBellMinistries.org

Made in the USA
Las Vegas, NV
31 October 2023